ABT

Outwitting
Clutter

OTHER BOOKS IN THE SERIES
AVAILABLE FROM THE LYONS PRESS

Outwitting Bears
Outwitting Critters
Outwitting Deer
Outwitting Neighbors
Outwitting Ticks
Outwitting Contractors
Outwitting Ants
Outwitting Poison Ivy
Outwitting Mice

Outwitting Clutter

Bill Adler Jr.

Series Concept Created by Bill Adler, Jr.

The Lyons Press

Guilford, CT

The Lyons Press is an imprint of The Globe Pequot Press

Contents

Introduction   **xi**

    What Is *Outwitting Clutter?*

    How to Use This Book

    What Makes Me the Big Expert?

1 Clutter and You   **1**

    Know Your Own Clutter-Tolerance Level

    Outwitting Clutter Clears the Mind and Strengthens the
       Body

    Clutter and Time

    Clutter Around the Clock

    Decluttering as a Creative Process

    What's Holding You Back?

2 Basic Decluttering   **19**

    Easy Clutter

    Not-so-Easy Clutter

    Getting Past the Denial Stage

    The Triage Method and How to Use It

    Mistakes Will Be Made

    For the Clutter-Intimidated: Start Small and Work Your
       Way Up to More Ambitious Things

    Who's Going to Help You?

    Take Advantage of Every Opportunity

    Label Spaces

    Brute Force

Make Friends with Strong Teenagers in Your
    Neighborhood
Dealing with Duplication
Defeat Clutter at Its Starting Point
Walk and Carry
Give Everyone Space
Indisputable Clutter: Stand Your Ground
Decluttering for Profit
Get Some Giveaway Friends

3   Clutter Around the House   **57**
Back to the Uncluttered Past?
The Stairs (and Other High-Priority Parts of the House)
Temporary Clutter
The Backs of Doors
The Safe-Place Problem
Room Decluttering: Two Strategies—Whole Hog or
    Piecemeal
Decluttering by Theme
The Kitchen: Its Most Common Clutter Problems Attacked
The Bathroom
Yard Clutter
How to Deal with Important Stuff You Think You Might
    Need Someday
Tools
Organize Neighborhood Giveaway Projects

4   Parenting and Clutter   **109**
Birthday Presents and Other Signs of a Cluttered but
    Happy Childhood
Newborn Clutter
Seven Strategies for Coping with Kid Clutter
Fast-Food Toy Clutter
Things to Put Kids' Things In

Assign Your Kids Outwitting Clutter Tasks
Chore Charts
Everything in Moderation

5 Clutter in All the Wrong Places   137
The Tough Stuff
Instruction Manuals
Hobby Stuff
Your Keys
Catalogs
Hair Stuff
Wallets and Purses
Car Clutter

6 Office Clutter   161
Starting from Scratch
The In-Box System
The "Touched-Paper" Rule
Fax Away Your Paper Piles
PIM to the Rescue!
Post-it Notes: Boon or Bane?
Business Cards
Changing Your Office's Clutter Rules
The End of the Workday
The Home Office
Messages and Reminders
Pay Your Bills Electronically

7 Digital Clutter   193
The Truth about Technology
Backing Up
Pruning and Organizing Your Digital Clutter
Keep an Archive
Preventing Digital Clutter

Friends Don't Let Friends Clutter Their
   Hard Drives

8 **Preventing Clutter**   213
Some Good Approaches to Preventing Clutter
The Barrier Method of Clutter Control
About Wedding Presents, Birthday Presents, and Other
   Unsolicited Gifts
Buy Things to Store Things
Yard Sales—The Path to Perdition
The Guest Room Problem (and How to Handle It)
Now That You've Outwitted Clutter, What Next?

9 **The Voices of Clutter: Interviews with**
   Real-World Experts, Victims, and Former
   Clutterholics   229
Joanne Helperin
Bob Farkas
Janet Kitto
Pat Moore
Suzanne Snyder

10 **The Top Ten Excuses People Give**
    Not to Declutter   239

Acknowledgments   244

Index   245

Introduction

What Is Outwitting Clutter?

I could put the main point of this book in eight words: *Get rid of stuff you don't really need.*

Then I would add a chapter or two to help you sort out those things that you really need from those that you can do quite well without. After that I would list the methods for organizing and storing the things you keep, so that your home and workplace would remain uncluttered. End of a very short book.

But that book could not be called *Outwitting Clutter.* That book would be your standard, off-the-rack how-to book. You've seen the type before, the "Do as I Say and not Only Will You Overcome Your Problem but You Will Become Rich and Sexy at the Same Time" self-help guide.

You know deep down what happens when you buy that kind of book. You read it through and get all fired up. "Yes, I can do that!" you say to yourself. "If I just follow all these steps, my clutter problem will be solved." So you begin to put into practice the author's advice. Maybe you start by clearing out your old newspapers (that was easy!); after that you tackle a small closet according to the instructions in the guide. Hey, not so bad. You're going along fine, maybe not as fired up as you were in the beginning, and then you come across a piece of advice that hits you like a brick. "Give away novels after you've read them." "Not my novels!" you object. "Then I'd never get to reread them whenever I felt like it. That's not how I want to live." Or maybe it's something that strikes you at first as quite a practical idea, until you try it out and discover it doesn't work for you at all. That prescription to deal with everything in your in-box the same day you receive it made sense on days when your in-box wasn't crowded, but then one day a crisis got dumped in your lap, and there was absolutely no way you were going to be able to fill out and mail those unimportant forms in your in-box and still keep that big project from collapsing around you. So you abandon the advice as unworkable in the real world, and pretty soon you're back to letting things pile up every day, just as they always used to do.

Well, that's not going to happen with this book. Sure, you'll find a lot of do's and don'ts in it, but with a difference. I'm telling you right here at the outset that you don't have to follow any set of rules—mine or anyone else's—to outwit your clutter problem. Following rules is not outwitting, it's being led by the nose. When you outwit something, you apply your own strategies, crafted to suit your own strengths and goals, to the particular types of clutter problems you find yourself up against in your own home or work environment. You wage war against clutter on your own turf, on your own terms. It isn't my purpose in this book to walk you through a series of steps, but rather to help you see what steps, in which direction, will be right for you.

In the chapters that follow you will learn to:

- Formulate anticlutter goals that make sense for your personality, lifestyle, living space, and workplace.
- Choose from among a wide variety of anticlutter strategies and tips.

- Look at some common clutter problems in an offbeat way.
- Come up with creative approaches of your own to get rid of clutter.
- Target areas of your home or workplace that are most important for you to declutter.
- Work in tandem (or at least not at cross-purposes) with other members of your family to tackle clutter problems created or exacerbated by more than one family member.
- Develop new anticlutter habits that you will be able to maintain in the future.

So in this book you won't find a section, for example, telling you how to install closet extenders, or build shoe racks, to deal with your clothing and shoe overflow. Instead I'll be talking about how you might begin to see the collection of shoes scattered near your front door in a new light . . . and, if you don't like that new light, give you a new and different idea about storing all those shoes in a place you hadn't thought of before. (Well, why should you have to pore through the book for that? Let me give you that right now, to save you some time. How about this: Buy a big, attractive wicker basket and place it by the front door. Toss all the most frequently worn pairs of shoes into it. The shoes are now kept where they're most often needed, and you're freed from having to try to enforce a frequently ignored rule about returning shoes to the shoe racks in the proper closet. You just grab any left-out shoes you find around the house and toss them in the basket. You've also freed up a lot of storage space in the closet for your less frequently worn pairs of shoes.)

For every solution, strategy, or option you will find in this book, I urge you to consider, "Is this something I should try? Or will it annoy me more than the annoyance of having that particular type of clutter around?" But if you try the solution and

find it doesn't quite work out as you'd hoped, you needn't go back to square one. Consider how you might vary the strategy or come up with some creative twist of your own that might make the solution fit under your own unique set of circumstances. By these means you will outwit your clutter problem, rather than substituting one problem (for example, not having as many pairs of shoes as you'd really like) for another (shoe clutter all over your house).

One other very important difference between *Outwitting Clutter* and other decluttering how-to books (and it's heresy to some professional organizers, but I'll say it without fear): *Some clutter is a good thing.* It's important to recognize that fact and learn to accept it. My goal is not to get you to throw out all but the inessentials in life. It's far more modest: to get you to be happy with whatever methods and strategies you adopt to sort through your clutter and keep it at a level that's comfortable for you and your family. If you set yourself an impossible goal, you'll give up before you accomplish anything worthwhile. But know what sorts of clutter you can live with and adopt practical methods of maintaining that level, and you will relax, face your decluttering chores squarely and without fear, and be able to see and deal with the clutter that's truly in your way.

How to Use This Book

Because this book is not the traditional do-this-do-that how-to book, you will notice that it isn't set up in the traditional step-by-step fashion. I don't tell you to start in the kitchen (for example) and cull the excess pots and pans first, then work on the dishes, and then the flatware, and move on to the pantry. Instead I present a smorgasbord of ideas, approaches, and techniques—usually more than one per clutter problem.

Some sections concentrate on types of problems (duplication; useless gifts given by people whose feelings you don't want to hurt), while others concentrate on specific areas (yes, I do tackle both the kitchen and the bathroom in separate discussions). I certainly won't shy away from including specific directives: "Nobody needs to save catalogs or old newspapers! Recycle them!" Let me stress, however, that these are my opinions. If you disagree, by all means ignore my advice. Mull over your own objections in your head, or voice them to other members of your household, but don't let the point end there. Let your reaction serve as your jumping-off place toward the creation of your own solution to the clutter problem of saved catalogs. For example, "If I limit myself to saving just the current version of my twenty favorite catalogs and keep them all stored in a single magazine holder—the sort that sits on a bookshelf—then I've got the catalogs I need, without letting them turn into clutter."

In addition to practical advice, you will also find lots and lots of anecdotes. Some are about people with far worse clutter problems than you. (Well, at any rate, I hope so.) They can serve as negative examples, or just give you a chance to reflect on how small your problems are by comparison. Some tell how someone solved a particularly tricky clutter problem in a clever or interesting way. And some are just tossed in to give you a chuckle now and again. Clutter has been known to bite back in funny ways. I also have found that outwitting clutter is best done with a dose of humor. Take it too seriously and you might feel it's nothing but a burden; you'll never even want to start.

Because the book isn't laid out in step-by-step fashion, I don't recommend you read it in any particular order. It's better to jump around to find what interests you. I believe one of the keys to outwitting clutter is to get yourself motivated to act. If you don't find inspiration in the section you're reading, move on quickly to another. Read with an eye to those notes that strike a chord with you, that sing to you, that make you want to get moving, to make happen what the words describe. If there's a particular clutter problem that you'd like to tackle first, then go to the table of contents, find the section dealing with that type of clutter, and get right to it.

All the while keep in mind that the rule for this book is *not* "Do as I say"—it's "Think about what I say and decide if it makes sense for you and your approach to clutter." You'll find a lot more in chapter 1 about how to evaluate yourself and your home in pursuit of attainable anticlutter goals.

What Makes Me the Big Expert?

Anytime you pick up a book filled with advice for handling a problem, you ought to wonder what makes the author qualified to tell you what to do. In many cases the question is answered by the author's academic or professional credentials. You buy a keep-your-dog-healthy manual and you expect the author to be a veterinarian. You buy an improve-your-golf-game guide because it's by some big-shot professional golfer you'd like to emulate. Makes sense, right?

Not necessarily, when the subject is clutter. The person who's an organizing genius, who seems to have been born with the neat-freak gene, may not be the right one to explain to you how best to reform your own bad cluttering habits. You'd probably be better off hearing from a naturally *dis*organized type, someone who learned through trial and error how to solve clutter problems and adopt good anticlutter habits that work, even for the most clutter-challenged among us. Someone who can warn you away from some organizing rules that don't work (or that might work only for the sort of person who's not constantly fighting the temptation to hang on to useless clutter).

What I'm saying here is that I am that person, a clutterer myself . . . reformed, of course. But not so reformed that I've forgotten how I used to let clutter pile up. I have the kind of insights into the mind of a clutterer that a person who's been well organized from the get-go could never have. You see, I've looked into some of those guides written by organizing maniacs . . . er, I mean, authorities . . . when I was trying to get a handle on my own bad cluttering ways. I read a few popular books, but I have to say, I found the systems described in books to be the sort that work only for someone with the same kind of neat-freak mind-set: Alphabetize everything; sort mail and other incoming documents the instant they turn up; buy storage racks and binders and specialized holders for every class of product you own and never let unlike items commingle. People who make fixed rules, people who need fixed rules. I'm not like that, and I suspect you're not either.

I outwitted my own clutter by ignoring or revising a lot of the typical rules I encountered. To strengthen my claim to success,

let me add that I was no slouch when it came to producing clutter. My house was crammed full of all kinds of junk before I decided to make some changes in my habits. I'm a writer and I
had the manuscripts for the twenty or so how-to books I've written on other subjects lying around the house, some of them in
multiple versions. (One of the first things I did was to pitch
them all; of course, I have computer versions saved on my hard
drive and several backups, some off site.) I'm also a parent of
two kids under age eleven, and as any parent can tell you, kids
and clutter go hand in hand. And without going into exact fig-
ures, let's just say I'm old enough to have acquired a great many
things in my time. And that's just *my* stuff I'm talking about; I'm
not even counting my wife's stuff. In other words, I had a full
houseload of clutter. Clutter that was getting in my way, keeping
me from finding things I needed when I needed them, not just
being too much of a good thing, but making me aware that clutter, once it's out of hand, turns into too much of a bad thing.
When I had that realization, I was determined to act, to conquer
clutter—but to do it in my own way.

So I turned away from the standard organizing guides and
set out to invent a new, more flexible approach. I wouldn't try to
eliminate clutter or micromanage the clutter but to outwit it—
that is, think up ways to deal with it that suit me, suit my house,
suit my family—even if it may not suit someone whose house
would pass Martha Stewart's standards of housekeeping.

I knew, too, that I could describe my methods to others, because I'd already had successes with many books telling readers
how to handle some familiar problems in an offbeat way. I started
with *Outwitting Squirrels* in 1988, which tackled the difficult question of how to organize your bird feeder in such a manner as to
feed the birds but keep the seeds away from those small, bushy-
tailed rodents that have nothing to do all day except try to invade

your feeder. I moved on to *Outwitting Critters, Outwitting Neighbors,* and *Outwitting Contractors.* The Outwitting series now has more than a dozen titles, with many more in the works. Of course, all of these other books deal with living things. You may think of clutter as inanimate, but I've learned that it actually shares some properties with other creatures. Like some of the animal pests I've taken on, clutter has a mind of its own. It's insidious and relentless. It can't simply be categorized out of existence—you'll do better to launch a sneak attack.

In the chapters to follow you'll learn how to take on your clutter by stealth, among many other ways. I'm still creating new ways myself as I continue the anticlutter crusade I started when I first realized that my clutter was in danger of taking over.

I should also add—or rather admit—that I haven't entirely vanquished my clutter problem. What I have done is cut it down to size; I've reduced it to the point at which I can maintain good control. It doesn't intimidate me anymore. I know that in the ongoing battle between clutter and me, I hold the upper hand. If ever it seems to be making a comeback, I can think up a new strategy before it scores a hit. That was my goal, and that I have certainly achieved.

Occasionally, I am called upon to step up my level of vigilance, and I launch into a frenzy of pruning and rearranging. Sometimes the old ideas stop working for me, and I go back to the drawing board. More often, I just need to tweak the old concepts a bit, refine them, adapt them to my changing clutter situation. That means occasional reassessment, reevaluation. I know I must never let myself become complacent.

It's good for me, I've learned, to keep rethinking, keep revising. It keeps my brain sharp and my house the way I like it. Our homes are so much a part of what we are, they're worth the effort it takes to keep them in tip-top shape. I think that as you apply the techniques in this book, you will discover the same. But at the risk of repeating myself too often, I caution once again, don't just do everything I recommend without thinking. Try out what you think will work for you, modify or amplify on whatever you think needs changing, and discard the rest. That's what outwitting clutter is all about.

Add your own creative ideas, too. If you come up with some clever strategy that keeps clutter at bay in your home or workplace, I want to hear about it. I might even include it, properly credited to you, of course, in a future edition of *Outwitting Clutter*. To contact me with your best Outwitting Clutter tips, visit my Web site www.adlerbooks.com and follow the links to "Outwitting Clutter/Leave an Outwitting Clutter Tip."

Clutter and You

Know Your Own Clutter-Tolerance Level

Before you can even begin to develop a strategy for outwitting clutter, you have to decide what it is you want to accomplish. You don't need all the details down, but you do need to have a general idea of what sort of solutions fit your personality, lifestyle, and family situation.

Why are you trying to outwit clutter? That is the first question you should ask yourself. If you are interested in a pure, completely clutter-free living space, as some people are, then you have to take one approach. If you can live with stacks of unread magazines, broken lava lamps, and a garden shed full of cracked flower pots, then your attitude has to be entirely different.

It's perfectly fine not to know your own clutter-tolerance level right now. Life is an exploration, an adventure. We change over time, and we change in different circumstances. And sometimes the courses that we pursue eventually lead us to conclude we're on the wrong path, and so we change tacks.

You are allowed, even encouraged, to try out different approaches until you find what works for you. Heaven forbid that you adopt a particular approach to clutter, say at the "neat-freak" end of the spectrum, then get married, have children, acquire pets, and still try to keep everything perfectly organized and devoid of any clutter. You're probably going to drive yourself and your family nuts.

So before you embark on any decluttering project, first take some time to step back and think about who you are, what you want out of life, what you think you'll want in the future, and what you think your family wants . . . and needs. Also, take into account the size of your home, how you currently use the space, and how you hope to be able to use it better. *Then* formulate your plan.

The first planning step is to acknowledge how you actually function in the real world. A good starting exercise is to take a look at how you have handled some project or other work that has created clutter before. If you haven't started or completed something in a particular period of time—a week, a month, whatever—will you ever do it? If that project is just sitting around and the truth is you're going to let the stuff sit around forever, it's better to acknowledge defeat and just get rid of what's causing clutter rather than force yourself to complete the project according to your earlier (now proven impractical) conception.

Unless you live alone, your decluttering plan must, in addition, take into account the cluttering habits of the others in your household. You need to know your spouse or boyfriend or girlfriend. Does your significant other like things neat and clean? Or are you the neater half of the equation? It's more likely that one partner is going to be a neat freak in a particular area, while the other feels the same way about a different area entirely. For example, I know a man who is an unbelievable slob at home but owns a car you could perform surgery in. There are other people who keep their living rooms clean and comfortable, but whose bedrooms could be taken for a dorm room at an all-jock frat house. Still others don't mind a messy kitchen, but can't stand to see a single toothbrush out of place in the bathroom. One person I know won't let you help clean up after dinner because she keeps her spices in alphabetical order, and doesn't trust anyone else to know the alphabet. (I'm not naming names, because I am actually related to this person by marriage and I don't want my wife to think I'm making fun of her mo . . . oops, I mean her unnamed relative.)

Your ultimate goal therefore must give due weight to everyone's various legitimate needs. And it can be frustrating to pursue an anticlutter mission if you're not clear on the parameters of that mission from the start.

It could be that in your particular case, your goal will be not to defeat clutter, but simply to learn to appreciate it. I realize that sentence may sound sacrilegious, but it's true: *Outwitting Clutter* may not be for you. Just as I have a chapter in my book *Outwitting Squirrels* called "What if You Like Squirrels?" I have to admit the possibility that you may actually like the clutter you live with. Well, to some degree we all do—or we wouldn't have let it accumulate in the first place. Unless you like living in a perfectly pristine environment with no mementos, reading materials, music recordings, postcards from friends, or toys of any kind around, you must have some clutter in your life. If you have children and try to live a clutter-free life, you're going to have to be on top of them all the time, and that could create problems in family relations that are far worse than the clutter problem you've cured. So strive for what is comfortable for you and the people who live with you.

Art or Objet d'Adolescence?

Dear Clutter Adviser:

I'm a big fan of horror movies and not just classics, like Nosferatu *and the original* Frankenstein. *I love those schlocky slasher movies with hockey-masked murderers or fiendish killer dolls. So when I came across an obscure catalog that had an original poster of one of my all-time favorites, I ordered it, expensive though it was. When the poster arrived, I was very excited. Then it dawned on me: I'm not fourteen anymore; I'm forty-two, and a gory horror movie poster just doesn't fit in with the way my wife and I have decorated the house. I can't bear to throw the poster out. What should I do?*

Signed,

Older than I Thought I Was

Dear Older:

Throw the poster out. I know—that's easy for me to say. But that's not what you want to hear, is it?

But let's assume that you're unwilling to waltz over to your trash can (your *outside* trash can, because using the outdoor trash can makes the poster less retrievable). You have a few options available. Can you hang the poster in your basement or garage? Or why don't you take the really bold step of framing the poster and hanging it someplace you'd enjoy seeing it. Isn't that what you bought it for?

Oh, but what about the wife? She's the one who doesn't think it fits in with the color scheme, isn't she? But surely there's some part of the house you can call your own. Do you have a home office? Or maybe a work corner? What about "your side" of the bedroom? After all, the house is half yours; there's got to be some wall space you can claim outright.

Now as to the argument that people over forty can't have horror movie posters: Stuff and nonsense! The moment you hang that framed poster on your wall, you've turned clutter into art. But just as there's no rule that says an adult can't hang a horror movie poster on the wall, there's also no rule that says that poster has to be displayed forever. When you tire of it, take the framed poster down and do one of these things:

- Sell it on eBay or some other online auction house.
- Give it to a kid who's the right age to appreciate the thing in all its beauty (and whose parents won't object to their child receiving such a gift).
- Throw it away in the outside trash.

And remember that this poster gave you pleasure for a while. But just as you may no longer find peanut butter and jelly sandwiches the kind of lunch you want to eat every day, so you may come to the realization that the poster isn't what you want permanently on your wall.

Outwitting Clutter Clears the Mind and Strengthens the Body

Zen and the Art of Outwitting Clutter

This could be an alternative title to this book, because it describes a side effect of outwitting clutter: a calmer, more relaxed life.

When I talk about the Zen of uncluttering, I don't mean specifically the positive benefits of living in a clutter-free household, because while it's true that less clutter often means less stress and anxiety, sometimes the effort of thwarting all clutter can be anxiety-producing. If you're hell-bent on getting rid of all the clutter in your house, you're going to turn an ultimately worthy goal into a miserable experience—and make everyone else around you suffer, too. So forget the ideal for now and concentrate on the process. Discover how the act of decluttering can become pleasurable and comforting. As you declutter, you make your life simpler. When you set yourself to reduce the clutter around you, you set aside (at least for the time being) far more stressful tasks, such as paying the bills or replacing the oil in your car.

Outwitting clutter puts you in a zone of reflection, self-awareness, and purification. It is also somewhat of a subconscious process. As you move things around your house, you achieve a more relaxed, almost transcendental state. Well, that's what you should be training your mind to do as you consider each object from a clutter-or-not point of view. What you definitely *don't* want to do is to let yourself get worked up about the process, getting into a mind-set that you *must* fix everything. Decluttering needs to be done at a calm, steady pace. Let yourself *enjoy* the act of decluttering. Don't look at outwitting clutter as a chore, but more as a way of ascending to a better state of being.

The 20-Minute-a-Day Way to Outwit Clutter and Lose Weight

Then there's the physical side of the activity. It almost goes without saying that you burn calories when you outwit clutter. The only way you can't get exercise is if all you do is shout at your kids or spouse to clean up their mess while you sit in front of the television. Almost any amount of decluttering by your own efforts will do good things for your health. To turn outwitting clutter into exercise, you should devote at least twenty to thirty minutes of continuous time to your anticlutter actions, and incorporate large, sweeping body movements whenever you can. The more moving, the better. Breathe correctly—deeply, from the diaphragm, as you move around. Why? If you're going to make your house more livable by getting rid of the clutter, you might as well do something to improve your own health at the same time. So work up a sweat!

Clutter and Time

Clutter reduces the amount of time you have to enjoy life by making it difficult to find things and by forcing you to climb over junk to get to what you want. When you're looking for a particular coat or pen or book or CD and there's a bunch of coats, pens, books, or CDs just piled up all over the place, you have to waste considerable time trying to find it. It's simple physics. Clutter is like a traffic jam—the stuff just gets in your way, slowing you down.

Clutter makes you waste time by making you fret about how to deal with clutter. Clutter creates a paralysis that renders you incapable of doing anything about the clutter. There's a never-ending dance that's going on between worrying about clutter and clutter causing you to worry. Like nail biting, it's a cycle that's hard to break.

Anyone who tries to outwit clutter eventually runs up against a certain thought process that says, "I just don't have the time to deal with this clutter." The antidote to that is to make more time by getting rid of those things that clutter up your time. If you're having trouble cutting into the clutter-time dance, deal with other things that waste your time, but that have nothing to do with clutter. If you can reduce the amount of time you waste on things not related to clutter, you'll feel calmer about approaching your clutter.

Telemarketers should come first on anyone's list of time wasters. Just say no and immediately put the phone down when a telemarketer calls. You can do the same thing with surveys that promise, "This will only take about twenty minutes." That's twenty minutes of time that belongs to you. (Occasionally surveys serve a public good, such as opinion polls; but most are conducted by businesses to help improve their marketing. Why should you donate your time to help a business make a profit?)

Lines. You can stand in line and get it today, or you can order *online* and get it in a few days. Trade standing in lines for ordering (as well as banking and bill paying) online. You'll save hours.

Time in traffic. Do you really have to drive your kids to and from school and soccer games every day? You'll have more time and your kids will have more time if you carpool and trade off driving with others who are going in the same direction (not to mention saving gas and wear and tear on your car).

Volunteering. You don't have to do it *every time* you're asked. When you really don't have the time to do a job the right way, you're actually doing your school, church, or community a favor by politely declining. If you say yes only when you can put in your best effort, you'll be a better volunteer. People who say yes out of pressure or a feeling of guilt tend to become resentful while they're working and less likely in the future to volunteer when they're really needed most. But limit your volunteering to those times when you can handle the extra work and your family can spare you, and you'll have your priorities straight.

Television. Turn the thing off a little earlier and get some sleep. Then you can wake up earlier and get more things done.

There are a zillion ways to snag a few minutes here and there. Attacking the problem of how to get the time to outwit clutter will give you all the time you need to outwit clutter.

Clutter Around the Clock

People often use the excuse, "I don't have enough time to get rid of clutter." And then they don't. A lot of us figure that if we can't manage to complete the project, it's a waste of time to even start. But I'm here to tell you: You're wrong. You *always* have enough time to accomplish *something*. To help prove this, I've devised this chart of things you can do in whatever time you have. You'll notice that even with increments of a little as *thirty seconds* you can accomplish something.

If you have . . .	*you could clean out . . .*
30 seconds	a coat pocket
a minute	the magazines in one magazine rack (just toss any old ones); a pen/pencil cup (toss all the broken ones)
5–15 minutes	a desk drawer; a kitchen cabinet; your underwear/sock drawer
an hour	a two-drawer file cabinet; your pantry shelves; the fridge or freezer
2 hours	a closet; a dresser; a desk
4 hours	a bedroom; the front hall closet; the family room/living room
6–8 hours (best if spaced out over a weekend)	the basement; the attic; the garage

Decluttering as a Creative Process

Decluttering your life does not mean that you should get rid of everything or anything in particular. When I talk about decluttering your life, I definitely don't mean blindly walking around your house and chucking stuff. Decluttering your house is a creative process. It takes imagination, tenacity, and ingenuity—plus time and attention, described above.

Often outwitting clutter isn't about throwing things out at all. (Nor is it about just putting things in a box in the garage or attic, either, so don't think you're going to get off easily!) Outwitting clutter could involve:

- Cutting down on quantity (do you need twenty-five pairs of shoes?).
- Reducing the size of some things (how about keeping your cereals in stackable bins instead of the original boxes?).
- Turning trash into treasures (selling things you no longer really want instead of just junking them).
- Finding new and different places to put stuff. (Instead of keeping your recyclables in the kitchen, put your covered recycling bin just outside the back door.)
- Periodically looking hard at your stuff. (After a time, much of our clutter becomes invisible to us, because we see it so often. Actually trying on your clothes now and then might reveal—sadly, I know—that those size 4s or 32 pants no longer fit and never will again.)
- Getting rid of clutter in unusual places. Many men happen to collect what could most kindly be called "damaged underwear." Tattered, torn, not the least attractive when seen by the opposite sex . . . well, you get the idea. This underwear is comfortable, to be sure, but this isn't the underwear you'd want to be wearing if you ever ended up in a hospital emergency room. (Here's a clever way to declutter your underwear drawer: Take the used underwear on a trip. Discard one each day after wearing. As your trip progresses, you'll get rid of underwear that's not fit for public viewing and declutter your suitcase at the same time.)

- Cultivating a new, outwitting clutter mind-set. (Think about setting a limit for your stuff: If you haven't touched it, used it, or thought about it for a year, then it's time to get rid of it.)

These are just a few techniques you can use to outwit clutter. Outwitting clutter is both a goal and a process. Unless you give up all your worldly goods to become a hermit in a cave, you will never be fully free of stuff. Indeed, many of your possessions are important, useful, or bring back pleasant memories. Less important than any of the actual tips in this book is its stress on learning how to make judgments and set priorities for decluttering that will let you live happily with the changes you'll make, rather than feel a sense of loss.

What's Holding You Back?

I used to think that most clutter was a result of laziness. It's easy to build a pile of paper, but its not so easy to organize that pile of paper, mostly because we don't want to. Let's face it, dealing with clutter is not fun. Who wants to spend the next two hours filing? Or cleaning a room? Or alphabetizing the spice rack? Or unpacking?

It's human nature not to want to take the time and effort to declutter. When was the last time you woke up and said, "I can't wait to straighten up the garage! I think I'll skip coffee and the newspaper and go right to it!"

The thing is, you know what's involved in doing what you have to do. Physical labor, moving heavy things from here to there. Boredom, reading through memos and old files and tax documents to decide if you need to keep them or move them someplace else or toss them in the trash. Anxiety, caused by the decisions you know you'll be called to make: Is this possibly broken breadmaking machine something we'll ever use again? Why did we stop using it—something went wrong with it, but what? If we got rid of it, who should get it? The charity shop? (But who's going to drop if off?) The trash collectors? Who needs these kinds of hassles?

These are all hurdles you must overcome, or rather outwit. In the chapters to come you'll find some useful—and maybe a few unusual—ideas about outwitting the physical labor, battling the boredom, and coping with the stress of decision-making involved in your decluttering efforts.

OUTWITTING CLUTTER TIP

You can get rid of clutter while you are completely naked. Think of this as an excuse to outwit clutter anytime. (Alternatively, you can imagine somebody else outwitting clutter while they are naked.)

Equal Partners/Unequal Clutter

Dear Clutter Adviser:

Perhaps you can help me. My wife leaves a lot of clutter around. For instance, she leaves her shoes all over the place—and she has a lot of shoes. She leaves catalogs on the kitchen table. She leaves her makeup stuff all over our sink. I have to admit that I contribute to the clutter in our house, but not nearly as much as she does. How can I get my wife to clean up after herself without having to devote "equal time" to my clutter? I don't want my request for Mary to clean up her clutter to lead to baseless recriminations.

Signed,

Happy Husband

Dear Happy,

You know that good marriage counseling costs $150 an hour, and if I answer your question here, you're getting a really good deal? Probably you don't. Most likely you think that your question has nothing to do with your relationship and everything to do with eliminating clutter.

But it's the other way around. And the way you've phrased your question shows that at least subconsciously you understand that. If this were just about clutter, you wouldn't be worried about the marriage equity issue; your wife's possible reaction to your quest wouldn't be a factor at all.

Any solution must take into account that there's a marriage at stake here. It's clear that Mary's shoe disorganization disease bothers you more than it bothers her—same for the makeup—so it's possible that your request will be met by a shrug and a "What's the big deal?" Not everybody sees the same things as clutter.

So what do I suggest? Just put her shoes in an organized place yourself. Same thing with her makeup supplies. But you've got to do it tastefully, in a way that your wife will appreciate; otherwise she'll get mad. Putting the shoes in a dark corner of your front hall closet and burying the makeup way in the back of the cabinet under the sink are not what I have in mind. You want to *improve* on what she's done, and show by demonstration that there is a better way.

You have to hope your wife will react by being pleased at the way you've worked to make her things both accessible and neatly organized for her. Then she'll cooperate in maintaining the system you've set up. But what if she objects to the swiveling multilevel shoe rack you've installed after great effort and some considerable expense? Don't hesitate to make her feel guilty for rejecting your chivalrous offerings. That's certainly a productive tactic (no matter what some $150-an-hour marriage counselor might have to say about it!).

The Top Ten Signs That You've Got Too Much Clutter

(With apologies to David Letterman)

10. You finally found the remote to the television, but it's the remote to the set that you got rid of five years ago.

9. You don't need to pack your car for a road trip—everything is still in there.

8. Sometimes you eat off a plate that says, 1964 WORLD'S FAIR.

7. You use your dishwasher to store your shoes.*

6. The eight-month-old *Newsweek* magazine at the doctor's office is recent compared to what you have at home.

5. When you reach into the back of your refrigerator for the milk, you get this strange feeling that something is in there, reaching for you.

4. You find yourself explaining to the emergency room physician how you impaled your foot on a Lego while tucking in your child for the night.

3. The Goodwill truck arrives at your house but the crew leader immediately calls "for backup."

2. You really think you might—just might, one day if you work out enough—fit into your favorite college pants that are still hanging in your closet.

. . . and the number one sign your life is too cluttered:

1. You have six or more copies of this book.

---

*For real: A New Yorker who always eats out and who has lots of shoes did this.

The Physical Properties of Clutter

Recent research into quantum mechanics has helped reveal some of the physical properties of clutter. Only when we have some understanding of the fundamental nature of the universe can we grasp the true significance of manifestations of clutter. Indeed, in some cases, it is the interposition of quantum mechanics and Einstein's theory of relativity that governs clutter.

Variable Visibility

Clutter is only visible to the naked eye under certain conditions. The producer of the clutter rarely has the ability to see it, although it may appear to take up double its volume to a viewer from a different perspective. In the home of the average person clutter has a tendency to blink away into an alternate universe, so that the resident is no longer aware it's there. On the other hand, a visiting in-law will be able to see even the most minute particle of clutter immediately upon entry.

Can this phenomenon be explained? Consider how the structure of space is affected by gravity. A sufficiently massive object, such as a star or black hole, will bend space, according to Einstein and others. This theory was proven when astronomers were able to view a star positioned behind the sun that should have been invisi-

ble without consideration of the space-bending effect. In the same way, clutter has been shown to be visible only to viewers who have a particular perspective from which to view it.

Spontaneous Generation of Clutter

It's also true that clutter is capable of spontaneous generation. Until the seventeenth century, when the Italian physician Francesco Redi demonstrated that maggots do not spontaneously emerge from rotting apples, people really believed that something could come out of nothing. But then, they also believed things like "The earth is flat." Not having at their disposal the scientific method that scientists rigorously apply today, it was generally assumed that clutter was the creation of a demonic imp or minion of the Evil One, who conjured it up in the middle of the night for the sake of confounding man and causing him to trip over things on the way to the bathroom in the dark.

Now, of course, we look for rational explanations of otherwise illogical phenomena. When clutter spontaneously appears, scientific minds are not content to ascribe its presence to supernatural creatures. They create hypotheses, which they then test under reproducible conditions. But consider a somewhat simplified account of what most physicists believe based on consistent test results: Something can arise out of nothing because of quantum fluctuations in the vacuum field. Quantum theory says that a vacuum is not entirely stable. All of the fields in the vacuum are constantly fluctuating. That's because there is no such thing as a pure vacuum—there is always some kind of energy activity in the vacuum. Energy and matter are intrinsically related, as Einstein proved with his famous equation $e = mc^2$. Matter gets converted to energy and vice versa. Because the vacuum of space is filled with energy, particles of matter are constantly being created. What are these particles? What purpose do they serve? We have no clear answer. To the human observer these particles appear as useless as clutter. Thus, clutter is what arises out of the nothingness of space.

At some point, under conditions that scientists are still unable to reproduce in the laboratory, these particles can coalesce into more substantial and familiar objects, such as paper clips, unusable pieces of exercise equipment, weird food in the back of the refrigerator, and an infinite variety of other shapes and forms.

But just because clutter can spontaneously emerge from a vacuum field doesn't mean individuals are not at fault, too. Much of the clutter gets brought home by somebody. One cannot blame Stephen Hawking for everything.

Clutter Multiplies

It's obvious to any observer that clutter has a mind of its own. It also has a drive for self-preservation, both individually and as a species. It seeks to reproduce and under the right conditions will multiply like bunnies.

How is it possible for an inanimate object to reproduce? In the same way one dust bunny or one cobweb turns into more. Pennies are also governed by the same physical phenomenon, perhaps requiring the National Institutes of Health to fund a multimillion-dollar study into the question.

Clutter Attracts Clutter

The moment there is clutter, it attracts more clutter. This is different from clutter reproducing. Clutter acts like a powerful magnet because clutter has dynamic static attraction, which causes any clutter nearby to be sucked in. When a person spies a cluttered place, he feels free to add to that clutter. Hence, what starts as single magazine or piece of junk mail can quickly and quietly become a giant pile, so big that it may have its own gravitational pull.

Clutter Appears to Be Many Times Heavier Than It Actually Is

Clutter just looks heavy. This is an optical illusion, one commonly caused by the interaction of a critical overabundance of separate, incompatible substances in the same pile. Gather some pens, paper, paper clips, shoelaces, broken eyeglasses, and batteries in the same space and it appears to be something so massive it can't be lifted. But clutter can be broken into its individual components, and in the process returns to the appearance of normal weight per item. That, however, does not solve the problem but merely shifts the illusion, because in the process of mentally separating the pile into its components, the concept of time becomes distorted. One no longer thinks of oneself as incapable of moving the pile; one becomes overwhelmed by the sense of the shortness of time available to complete the project. It now appears that it will take eons to transport each individual item to its proper place. This phenomenon of clutter is known as the Mass/Time Shift Paradox.

OUTWITTING CLUTTER TIP

If you don't know where to start, start with a desk drawer or cabinet. It's easy to declutter a single space than to tackle a large room or an entire house.

Basic Decluttering

2

Easy Clutter

Let's start with easy clutter. What do I mean by easy clutter? These are things that you can *always* throw away, such as bent paper clips and dead batteries. Easy clutter, however, needs to be dealt with promptly, or else it will turn into actual, permanent clutter. Dealing with easy clutter requires a small bit of foresight and a modicum of willpower—after all, the simplest thing of all is to do nothing about each new bit of clutter that creeps into your home.

Here's a list of things that can be immediately thrown away, no questions asked. Feel free to add items of your own:

- Dead and dying batteries.
- Lip balm with so little balm left that you have to scrape your lips along the top of the tube to put it on.
- Toothpaste tubes that have turned into grip exercise machines, because you have to squeeze them to death to get any toothpaste out.
- Broken paper clips, bent safety pins, headless thumbtacks.
- Toys with terminally missing parts.
- Dead pens, leaky pens, or pens with unreliable ink flow.

- Pens that are missing their caps.
- Caps that are missing their pens.
- Crayon nubs.
- Notes that no longer make any sense.
- Business cards from people you don't do business with anymore.
- Keys that really, truthfully don't fit anything anymore.
- Keys to ex-girlfriends' or ex-boyfriends' apartments, even if they do fit.
- Petrified Silly Putty and Play-Doh that no longer plays.
- Any more than two shoe boxes, egg cartons, or take-out food cartons.
- Expired drugs.
- Unexpired drugs that caused you side effects or didn't work to solve your problem.
- Dull razors.
- Records and CDs that are just too scratched to play.
- Tapes that have pulled out of their cassettes.
- Holey shoes, holey socks.
- The last scrap of gift wrap on the roll that's clearly too small to wrap anything but a microbe in.

Outwitting easy clutter also involves some stealth: How exactly do you get rid of the combination hot dog bun and hot dog cooker that your parents gave you without insulting them?

Admittedly, both of the following rules are stumbling blocks when it comes to outwitting easy clutter, but I wouldn't call it "easy clutter" if I didn't think you could quickly train yourself to get around them. Just let me plant a few firm thoughts in your brain, the first of which is: **DON'T BRING IT HOME!** I taught myself this one out of professional necessity. I'm in the book business and consequently I get books from publishers all the time. Occasionally it's just too awkward to say "no thanks" to a book, and when I can't, I have to leave the publisher's office with a book in hand. (More accurately, it's a bag o' books.) What to do? If you're a publisher who has ever presented me with a collection of your company's finest works, please don't read any farther. I've never had any trouble finding people wandering the downtown streets who are only too happy to take a free book or two and save me from bringing them home to gather dust on my shelves.

Look, you have a choice here. You can take a positive, proactive step to keep something from becoming clutter, or you can be a wimp. It's up to you. My personal feeling is that if you take home something you don't really want (do you actually need that AM radio the bank gave you?) then you're going to fail at 99 percent of the other decluttering tasks I'm going to assign you. This one is so basic, so elemental to outwitting clutter, that's it worth repeating: DON'T BRING IT HOME!

The second, and slightly more difficult command to get hardwired into your brain cells is: **CHUCK IT!** If you find it difficult to throw out things that someone else might consider useful, just think of the most likely alternative: You do nothing, and the clutter will remain with you, possibly for your entire life. Like jumping into a cold lake or swimming pool, the only difficult part is summoning the nerve. The leap itself involves no effort, since gravity does all the work. Dump it, make it disappear. As long as our street corners have large trash bins on them, the only thing holding you back is your mind. (Still too chicken to actually put something that may have value to someone in the trash bin? Drop it off at charity-run thrift shop.)

Here're some more types of easy clutter for you to practice on:

Used car parts. Are you going to study the parts and maybe decide that the car repair shop didn't do the right thing? Here's what to do: Thank the shop guy for saving them for you, glance at them as if you can see in an instant why they needed to be replaced, and then add casually, "You can get rid of 'em for me now."

Catalogs, magazines, and newspapers. Do you really need to keep catalogs filed alphabetically—meaning, do you really need to keep those catalogs at all? Recycle them along with magazines, newspapers, and any other papers that may be picked up at curbside in your local area or may be dropped off at nearby collection points. Give up the newspaper clipping system you developed many years ago. Everything's available online these days—and have you *ever* consulted those articles you saved?

Recipes. Collecting them was fun, but haven't you learned to make the good ones from memory? All the rest just take up space.

Books. Do you keep a mini shelf of books on your night table or, worse, on the floor beside your bed? Do you keep a stack of magazines on your coffee table? More to the point: If you only read one book at a time, and if the same thing goes for that stack of magazines, isn't it time to rethink the whole book- or magazine-stacking system?

Clips and fasteners. Do you save paper clips and butterfly clips that arrive with incoming mail? If you use those clips, then that's a good practice; if you never use them, toss them without another thought.

Pennies. Penny jars may seem like a good way to keep pennies from turning into clutter, but if you have more than one jar, you've got a jar clutter problem. Consolidate down to one jar, and then empty the jar on a regular basis. Many grocery stores have a coin-counting machine that lets you dump in your loose change and get paper money in exchange—minus a nominal fee.

Boxes. Not only should you challenge the old ways of thinking about *what* you keep, but *where* is something you should reevaluate, too. Let's say you have a burning need to hold on to shoe boxes. I won't question your motives, but do you need to keep all those boxes in your closet? Isn't a closet supposed to be for clothing, not boxes? Maybe there's a better place for the shoe boxes, such as the attic, basement, or where you keep your gift wrapping stuff or your art supplies.

How many things do you have around that are either "for just in case" or are in your house because that's the way you've always done it?

Not-so-Easy Clutter

I've talked about the things that virtually anyone would recognize as clutter. Let's move on now to something a bit harder: broken things that are clearly fixable. Of course you know that if a thing is broken but not fixable, it's clutter. Get rid of it. But when you can see that a thing would be useful again if fixed, then the question becomes, "Is it worth fixing?" If the answer to that is no, then it's still clutter, and you should throw it out or give it away to someone who likes to fix broken stuff. If the answer to the question is yes, then waste no time in getting the thing fixed, because as long as it sits there waiting to be fixed, it's still clutter.

On to yet a harder level: Consider the things that at one time you loved, but now hardly ever use. Maybe it's some article of clothing that no longer fits. (You know what I'm talking about here.) I find that a good clutter-beating guideline is to set a time limit for such objects. If I haven't worn it, touched it, used it, or especially thought about it in a year, two at the outside, then I make myself get rid of it.

It's important not to go overboard, though. I once read an article about clutter that said, "Get rid of those old photos of Uncle Albert. Get rid of your old school papers—nobody, not even you, wants to look at them again." I happen to disagree strongly. Memories are what hold our souls together. If you have a happy childhood, chances are you will be happy as an adult. When you begin to get stressed or conflicted as a grown-up, it is your childhood memories—the days bicycling with your parents, turning your bedcovers into a tent, seeing a rainbow for the first time—that bring you back into balance. And sometimes these mementos of our past—clutter by another name—can help us remember the good old days. In large measure we are our memories.

So what am I doing here, recommending that you actually *keep* stuff that exists in that twilight zone between junk and valuable? Notice that I'm not saying you keep *everything*—every school paper, every picture, every art project, every baseball game program, every school textbook. Just keep some of those things, the meaningful ones. The ones that bring back the good times (or not-so-good, but historically important); the ones you want your children and grandchildren to know you by. By having fewer of them, the meaningful mementos become even more significant.

Photos of Old Flames

Dear Clutter Adviser:

What do I do with pictures of my old girlfriends? I don't really need them anymore, but I don't want to throw them out, either.

Sincerely,

Nostalgic Ned

Dear NN,

Why? What for? Why do you want to keep these pictures?
No. Don't answer that.

If you're absolutely, 100 percent certain that you want to keep these pictures, put them in some waterproof box, label that box NED'S PAST, and place the box in a distant corner of your attic, basement, or garage. I presume that your wanting to keep these pictures has something to do with your looking at them ten, twenty, or fifty years from now; or maybe you want your grandchildren to see them. If that's the case, be sure to label who's who. I'm not commenting on the amount of social activity you've had; it's just that over time memory fades, and without a "who's who" you might as well have a box filled with pictures cut from *Vogue.*

(If you want to have a little fun with your descendants, toss in a few pictures of Christie Brinkley, Margaret Thatcher, and Katie Couric. Let your grandchildren speculate.)

You might consider sending the pictures back to your exes, too. Chances are that you have some photos of Boopsy that Boopsy would love to have. You can either pop the pictures in the mail, or give that ex a call and ask if she'd like some old pictures. If you're afraid to throw out the pictures because they are a link to your past, then use the pictures to reconnect to your past and give her a call. Or is that *really* what you're afraid of? Think it over, and you might find out.

Getting Past the Denial Stage

Denial is perhaps one the most entrenched clutter problems people have. Every day people open their closet doors and just don't *see* all the suits and dresses that they no longer wear.

(Yes, those little tailor fairies have been very busy taking your clothes in a notch or two while you sleep.) Denial is what's going on every time you open your desk drawer and notice the loose change, but not the old keys that open no locks. Your brain has the ability to block off the part of its memory bank that holds the image of the useless object you'd rather not have to deal with. That's how that five five-and-a-quarter-inch floppy disc that's been sitting on your desk (that your computer no longer even has a slot for) can remain in place, useless, year after year.

You need to force yourself to see clutter. You need to walk up to that big closest, fling open the doors, and say out loud to yourself (and members of your family, too), "This closet sure is cluttered!" You need to go outside your house and then walk back in through the front door and look around, with fresh eyes, as if you've never been there before. Examine with a critical eye objects that you might have assumed were useful, putting aside all prejudice and wishful thinking (like, "I need forty coffee mugs for that huge neighborhoodwide brunch I'll throw someday.").

Not everyone can do this unassisted. Sometimes your family members or close friends need to help you see the reality you simply cannot face head-on. If anyone close to you has ever complained to you about your clutter, don't be offended; enlist that person's aid in the exercise of viewing your living situation through another pair of eyes. Invite that person to walk through your home with you, pointing out whatever appears to him or her to be clutter. Ask your clutter critic to be brutally honest. A person who doesn't care about you will generally decline the responsibility involved in this task; the person who accepts the challenge has demonstrated a concern for your welfare. Remember this as you absorb the person's observations and comments, however negative they may be. Whatever

Does your closet look like this?

you hear, don't get mad—that's counterproductive. The final thing to keep in mind is that you don't *need* to act on any of the person's anticlutter suggestions. Your aim is to open your mind to a different point of view, not to empty your mind of your own opinions.

OUTWITTING CLUTTER TIP

The moment you find yourself putting a book or magazine on a bookshelf horizontally is the moment you've lost the clutter war.

The Triage Method and How to Use It

The first thing you need to do is make a mental checklist. As you examine each item from a clutter-or-not perspective, ask yourself these questions:

- Is it important? (Prescription drugs, yes; a recipe for candy corn, no.)
- Do I love it? (Your high school yearbook, yes; a torn souvenir T-shirt from ten years ago, no.)
- Do I need it? (A wrench, yes; a Barney sippy cup when your children are now past the legal drinking age, no.)
- Does it make my life better? (A programmable coffee machine, yes; a cigar humidor, no.)

Once you've asked these questions, move to the next step: Organize or sort your stuff by priority. Things that are essential go at the top of the list, things that make your life better go toward the bottom of the list, and things that don't make the list at all have got to go. (There are exceptions, so please, as always, be flexible when interpreting my recommendations.) You can use different-colored Post-it notes to mark things if you want, or you can sort your stuff into three boxes.

Box 1: I really need it, love it—and it still functions.

Box 2: I like it, and it could be of use (it still works). But I might not need it and perhaps could give it away or throw it away.

Box 3: It may still work, but I didn't even know that I still owned it and haven't used it for a long time; *or* It doesn't work and can't be made to work and so should definitely go.

This type of sorting process is known by the term *triage*. The same term is used in emergency rooms to describe the process by which doctors decide who needs lifesaving measures, who can wait for less-than-urgent medical care, and who is beyond help. Although triage as a means to treat clutter does not deal with life-or-death questions (well, not normally), it does have bearing on both your physical and mental health, and so the term is fitting.

Now, once you have triaged all the stuff that's plain broken or not useful or desirable into Box 3, get rid of that box! On to Box 2: Perhaps as much as 75 percent of what's in that box can be thrown out or given away. You'll have to ask yourself some hard questions about each item. "If I did keep it, when would I use it? How often? Where would I keep it when I'm not using it? If I got rid of it, would I ever miss it? Why? Wouldn't someone else get more out of having it? What's the trade-off between clearing it out and having the space, and keeping it and having the object for its intended use?" Assign point values to your answers, if that will help you analyze the situation in each case and come to a rational decision.

Finally, what's in Box 1 you have my permission to keep. But you get awarded bonus points for throwing or giving away anything that's in Box 1.

Mistakes Will Be Made

When considering our clutter, at one point or another, we've all had the same thought that this homeowner has:

> *"Sometimes I almost wish a fire would sweep through my home, thereby stripping me of the need to make decisions and to act."*
> —Anonymous posting on an e-mail list about clutter

But then you have to remember that a lot more would be swept away than the clutter and the need to make decisions. You'd lose your whole house, too. I'm afraid there's just no getting around the fact that once you decide to declutter, you're going to have to make decisions about things. It's fine to take your time over some of the things to give away. There's no law that says decluttering has to be fast and dramatic. It can also be done at a slow, steady pace. Generally speaking, doing so results in more thoughtful and deliberate actions, leading to an even more uncluttered result.

The fear of getting rid of something you actually might later need should never deter you from your decluttering goal. It's possible—you might actually need the old stuff—but only as long as you continue to worry about every conceivable circumstance that could come along. Then again, as long as you worry about whether or not you'll need your clutter, it will remain where it is, preventing you from accomplishing your goal.

The truth is that you *will* make a few wrong decisions when dealing with clutter. It is inevitable. But these decisions will be small wrong decisions. By way of example, forgetting to lock the front door before a long trip (oh no, have I created a new worry for you?!) could be considered a relatively big and bad decision. Throwing out a bunch of T-shirts and sweatshirts and then realizing that you need one because your son's friend's shirt got soiled during a touch football game is a lot different. Once you acknowledge the fact that every decision carries a bit of risk, you'll be better at assessing the risks and making the right choice in each case.

Always remember—it's only *stuff*. Stuff can be replaced, or if it can't, you can substitute something else for what you later realized you got rid of by mistake. For instance, let's say that the sweatshirt you gave to Goodwill was an old, favorite college sweatshirt with your college logo on it, and weeks after you gave it away you woke up in a cold sweat in the middle of the night, realizing that you'd made a terrible mistake. Can that mistake be rectified? Can you get your sweatshirt back? No, obviously not. But you can do other things, such as ordering a brand-new sweatshirt from your school with the same logo. Or you can find a picture of yourself wearing that sweatshirt and put the framed picture on the wall.

Regretting a clutter decision often has as much to do with nostalgia as it does with practicality. That sweatshirt might have been useful one day—if all the others you have were dirty—but the real regret stems from your not realizing how important it was to you until after it was gone. The odd thing about this sentimental feeling you now have about your college sweatshirt is that you didn't feel this way until you gave the sweatshirt away. It was the act of decluttering that moved you to feel emotional about the sweatshirt. If you still possessed the sweatshirt, you would probably regard it as annoying clutter. If you take a moment to think about what's happened, throwing away this sweatshirt has brought to the surface feelings in you that were dormant. You may have lost a shirt, but you've gained memories and emotions that are possibly more dear.

"I retrieve the memories quickly as I can and add them to the portrait we all draw in our minds."
—Vienna Teng, songwriter (www.viennateng.com)

For the Clutter-Intimidated: Start Small and Work Your Way Up to More Ambitious Things

A journey of a thousand miles starts with a single step. So the ancient Chinese saying goes. True, but if you fly, you don't have to take any steps at all!

Let's assume for a moment that you don't have a professional organizer visiting your home on a regular basis—the clutterer's equivalent of flying first class. (You can always solve a problem by throwing money at it, and hundred-dollar bills are one of the few things that never seem to create clutter.) Let's assume also that the clutter stops here. With you. Just as every family has a person who's generally in charge of the laundry, driving the kids to soccer, cooking dinner, and repairing a broken light switch (and it's not supposed to be the same person for all these jobs!), there's generally one person who's in charge of clutter. (I will explain how you can go about acquiring a willing anticlutter volunteer a little later on.) With no helpers, how can you possibly keep a handle on clutter? It's easy to feel overwhelmed.

The answer is that if you take care of the little things, the big ones will fall into place. When it comes to clutter, it's often a case of the accumulation of many small items of clutter that causes your whole home to seem more cluttered than it is, and that makes you feel as if you are surrounded by clutter. For instance—and this may sound somewhat familiar—on my desk right now are a computer, monitor, and keyboard. I need the computer, monitor, and keyboard to write this book. Also on my desk is the remote control to the stereo, so I can listen to music instead of writing this book. I've got a roll of Scotch tape, a calculator, a Palm Pilot, three coasters, an empty prescription bottle that I had on my desk so I could call the pharmacy for a refill (and, no, I'm not going to tell you what it's for), a flashlight, a telephone, a set of keys to my parents' apartment in New York, a luggage lock, three mugs filled with pens, pencils, rulers, screwdrivers, styluses for my Palm Pilot, and a couple of pairs of scissors, a Web cam for doing video conferencing, a little snake sculpture, a deck of cards, a pocketknife, multiple Post-it notes with messages scribbled on them, a whistle, an empty glass that once contained water, an empty coffee cup that recently was filled with coffee and needs to be refilled, another coaster (which I just spotted), two pens, and a small stack of Zip discs.

I'm sure that my desk is not perfectly typical, but in some ways it is quite typical: There's a fair amount of clutter on it. There's stuff on my desk that just doesn't need to be there.

That's obvious: I hardly need the three pen-holder mugs, since I rarely need more than one or two working pens, a Palm Pilot stylus, a ruler, and a screwdriver, all of which can fit quite easily into a single pen-holding container. (I certainly don't need a pencil with an eraser, since I don't ever make miztakes that need to be corected.) I don't need four coasters—two are more than enough. I *know* that if I looked at the twenty or so Post-it notes, more than three-quarters would be so old that the area codes for the messages would have changed since I first wrote the note. The whistle? I have no idea what it's doing on my desk, but there it's been for a long time. The deck of cards ended up here, I think, after an interminable game of War with my seven-year-old daughter, Claire. I don't need to go through the entire inventory, but you get the idea. There is a lot of clutter on my desk.

I'm not going to walk you through every single step I took when I decluttered my desk—you don't need that level of detail. What I want to illustrate here, and which you've probably guessed from the heading, is that it's not necessary to deal with a clutter problem all at once. You can tackle it bit by bit. Here's how I would rip through my messy desktop: The whistle can go in the basement closet with my camping stuff. In less than five minutes I can deal with all those excess Post-it notes. (Either I already bought my wife that necklace for our most recent anniversary, in which case I definitely don't need the Post-it reminder from the jewelry store that it's come in, or I didn't get her the necklace, in which case I'm really in trouble.) In fact, I can deal with *all* of them, by entering whatever scant information I actually do need into one of the various note-taking programs on my computer. Four coasters get turned into one by means of a quick dropping-off of three to the living room, where they are needed. The Web cam that I've never used for video conferencing (seemed like a good idea when I bought it) would do a lot more good mounted to my front door frame to scare away potential burglars. And so on. The point is that it takes just a moment or two to deal with clutter if you look at your clutter as many small projects rather than one intimidating, all-or-nothing job.

Who's Going to Help You?

In any environment, enlist the help of the person in your household who is most clutter-averse. You'll probably find that the person in your family who hates clutter the most (other than you, or perhaps more than you) is very happy to help you with your efforts. As with many things, decluttering is more fun when two or more people are involved than when you're flying solo. Often people never get started on a decluttering effort because they don't feel up to tackling it alone.

It may be that the shoe situation downstairs bothers you, while the bathtub shelf piled high with toys is what bothers your spouse. Make a deal: She helps you organize the shoes, and you help her put away the toys. You may find that with a partnership you get to outwit even more clutter than you thought possible.

Take Advantage of Every Opportunity

Taking advantage of every opportunity to declutter your house doesn't mean that you're working 24/7* to outwit clutter. Heaven forbid! You certainly need some time during the year to do fun stuff, like mowing the lawn and filling out your 1040.

What I'm actually suggesting is that you turn ordinary activities into times to outwit clutter. Every time you get something new or put something somewhere, spend a moment to evaluate the clutter situation. For example, when you plug something new into an outlet or multi-extension cord, ask yourself if everything that's plugged in actually needs to be there. I've found that with power cords, if you follow the trail from the outlet outbound, you often discover that there's nothing at the other end. While you're looking underneath for the outlet, see if there's any clutter down there that can be gotten rid of.

Are you putting a new car registration card in your glove compartment? Take a minute or two to see what's in your glove compartment, besides the old registration card, that can be thrown out.

Buying a new book? Why not triage your bookshelf for novels that can be given away?

Acquiring some new CDs? Isn't it time to give away *The Best of ABBA*?

---

*For the record, this is the first time I have ever used the expression *24/7*.

As you put your new, sharp steak knives in the drawer, you might think about transporting the old, dull ones from that same drawer to the scrap heap. Hanging on to the old, worn steak knives is just going to make it harder to find the new, good ones.

Buying new clothes gives you the opportunity to make more room in your closet by getting rid of *all* the old clothing that now longer fits or has large purple polka dots on it.

When you purchase your new car, that's an excellent opportunity to remove all the old flashlights and jumper cables from your old auto and call the Salvation Army to haul it away. (Don't forget, you can legally deduct the "book value" of the car, even if you know in your heart it's close to worthless.)

This is one of the most practical ways to outwit clutter. In many ways, replacing old things with new things is easier than simply throwing stuff out. When you get something new, it's less painful to throw out the old model (spouses excepted) than it is to simply throw away something without replacing it. Conversely, it's important to recognize that you're on the road to a real clutter problem, the opposite of outwitting clutter (creating what I will call "dimwit clutter"), if you don't get rid of the old stuff at the same time that you get new things.

Phone books and almanacs are good examples: Why do you need the 2001 phone book when it's now 2002?

Every time you fiddle with some part of your house or office, think of it as an opportunity to outwit clutter, and soon these actions will become a habit, with little or no thought involved. Your clutter problems will lessen gradually over time, until one day you look around and realize you no longer have to work at your clutter problem but just keep up the automatic clutter disposal patterns you have trained yourself to adopt.

OUTWITTING CLUTTER TIP

It's perfectly fine to do a partial job of decluttering a room. After all, a little less clutter is always better.

Label Spaces

Get that label maker out. I have a job for you. I want you to label various places in your house—cabinets, drawers, bookshelves, closet shelves, attic areas, basement cabinets, CD racks, anything and everything. Label spaces with words and phrases like BATTERIES, COMPUTER CABLES, PHOTO NEGATIVES, COSMETICS, HOLIDAY CARDS, GIFT WRAP, SCHOOL PROJECTS, SHOELACES, CAMPING SUPPLIES, TRAVEL GEAR, FIRST AID, DIAPER STUFF, and so on. This will inspire you to put things in their proper place. And it will help you keep to a working system. As a bonus, labeling spaces might get other people in your family to start putting things away where they belong, too.

This system only works with things that share a common function. ELECTRICAL SUPPLIES works, for instance; labeling a shelf GADGETS won't be as effective. Once you've labeled a certain space, make sure everyone in your house understands clearly what belong there. Unless you explain why you've taken the time to type out letters on a labeling machine, your spouse and children may choose to ignore the new system.

You may need to offer persistent reminders about how the system works in the beginning. But I think you'll find as the system matures and develops that by labeling, and occasionally relabeling spaces, as needed, you have crafted a working, permanent solution to many forms of clutter.

Runaway Remotes

Dear Clutter Adviser:

We have a television, VCR, CD player, cable box, and DVD in our family room. That makes for quite a collection of remote controls. We bought a so-called universal remote to avoid having to play with four remotes just to watch Survivor. *But the universal remote isn't so universal; it seems that we still need one of the other remote controls to perform a single function, such as changing the volume on the television. What can we do about all these remotes that are cluttering our family room?*

Signed,

Awfully Cluttered/Digitally Challenged

Dear AC/DC,

First, don't do what I did—continue searching for the perfect universal remote. As far as I can tell, there isn't one, and all that's going to happen if you try to buy a new, improved universal remote is that you'll have one more remote that's just clutter.

If you were starting anew, I'd suggest buying electronics made by the same company—that way you at least have a chance of one remote working everything. But I gather it's too late for that.

Part of your clutter problem may related to not being able to quickly identify which remote is which. The TV and VCR remotes probably look the same, especially in a darkened room. By labeling your remotes it will be easier to grab the one that you actually need to make the device do what you want. You may be able to outwit remote clutter just by organizing it.

If labeling doesn't work, then color-code your remotes with different-colored electrical tape; or you can use stickers to make it easy to quickly identify the remote you're looking for.

I've also seen various designs of remote control holders. If your remote control clutter is severe enough a problem, consider buying one. Alternatively, you could purchase an over-the-door shoe holder and keep your remotes in that.

Brute Force

Sometimes you need to attack a particular clutter problem with brute force. No sly, cunning, clever techniques; just hard, physical labor. Lifting, moving, bagging. There's not a whole lot I can say about that, other than you won't have to do it all the time, but on those occasions when you're scratching your head looking for a crafty way to deal with clutter and can't find that way, it's probably because none exists. Looking for an ingenious solution only delays the inevitable.

Still, there are some tips I can throw your way that may help. When you have a lot of clutter that simply needs to be moved somewhere, the hardest part of the process is preparing the space where the clutter goes. This isn't really a problem when it's the sort of clutter that gets thrown out (bagged yard trash, for example), but it is when it's the sort that must be put somewhere, like last year's tax files. In case of an IRS audit, you must hang on to your records and documents for at least the last five years. Unless you have that somewhere prepared in advance, you're not going to be able to outwit clutter in any meaningful way. Let's say you want to empty a bookshelf. Some of your books can be thrown away or given away, but others you may want to move. Perhaps you have some coffee table picture books that you want in the living room. If there's no free space in the living room, though, moving these books at all will only be a frustrating experience. Or you may want to transport some CDs from your family den to your home office—but if there's no shelf space in your home office, the CDs may just end up piled on the floor.

Well, that's at least better than the worst-case scenario when dealing with clutter by brute force, which goes like this: You gather up those heavy boxes of old papers that you're moving out of your home office, intending to put them in the basement. To avoid making two trips up and down the stairs, you're carrying several heavy boxes at once, stacked one on top of another. You stagger under the load. You manage to make it safely down the stairs, across the rec room floor, and into the storage area. And then you realize what's wrong: There's not an inch of floor space available to put the boxes down. But they're heavy, and you don't think you can keep them balanced in front of you for another second. Maybe you can rest them on that old, rusted TV table? Down they go. But the table won't bear the weight. Oh noooo! Crash! The boxes turn over and everything spills out all over the floor . . . except there's no floor space available, so the papers are actually spilling all over the other boxes, broken pieces of furniture, and everything else piled high in the storage room. And all because you didn't take the simple precaution of checking to see where you'd put the stuff before you hauled it down.

Make Friends with Strong Teenagers in Your Neighborhood

Let me tell you a story. It's a short story and, I'm sorry to say, a dull story. But the story does have a point, so I'm going to tell it.

I was cleaning out my office and brought home an old computer and monitor to let a friend borrow. That's a good way to deal with clutter: Something that you can't use, somebody else may find useful. So, with some effort, because computers and monitors are both heavy, I trucked the equipment home, where my friend was going to meet me to pick them up. It turned out that Steve needed only the computer—he had his own monitor. That meant I was left with a twenty-five-pound computer monitor in the front hall of my house, and no place to put it.

My back was already a bit sore from bringing the computer home, so I didn't want to haul the monitor back to my office, and I didn't have anyplace in our house to keep it. The thing I least wanted to do was attempt to pick up the huge monitor (this one had a nineteen-inch screen, the really super-duper size) and carry it up two flights of stairs to the attic. So there the thing sat—for more than two months—until I finally heard about a friend of a friend who needed just the monitor.

Only later did I realize what I could have used at the time—a strong teenage friend. If I'd had a buddy-buddy relationship with some well-muscled sixteen- or seventeen-year-old in the neighborhood, my problem would have been gone in no time. Teenagers always can find something to do with any working piece of computer equipment. Even if they can't use it themselves, they're connected to schools and lots of other organizations that are always looking for all kinds of things for their annual this-or-that drive. And even if they can't find some worthy cause to take the computer, at the very least they're young and strong enough to haul almost anything up the stairs for you.

The question is: How do you befriend a teenager? For a forty-something-year-old man, the answer doesn't come easily. I don't exactly share their usual taste in music or other entertainment.

In fact, most of my conversations with the teenagers who live nearby have up to now been limited to asking them to turn down the volume on the music blaring out of their car radios. But I'm now working on discovering what we have in common. So far the best I can come up with is a shared interest in the health of the American economy. It seems to me that they're all really into boosting consumer confidence by spending a lot of money on stuff. But for them to pursue this activity, they have a constant need for extra cash. That's something I can help them with. I can pay them for odd jobs around the house—not just lawn mowing and baby-sitting, but also semiskilled work, such as small painting projects and assembling bookshelves. Then, after I've established a regular relationship with a friendly, hardworking kid, I stand a good chance of being able to invite him or her over for a soda one afternoon and casually drop a remark along these lines: "See that computer monitor in the front hall? It's too heavy for me to move to the attic. Do you think you might be able to give me a hand with it?" and have the kid respond, "No problem, man," without feeling taken advantage of.

Once you've got your teenage buddy/hired helper, you can also enlist his or her aid (fairly compensated, of course) in the physical labor of decluttering a garage, basement, or attic.

Dealing with Duplication

This clutter problem may also be called "too much of a good thing," and it can prevent you from enjoying things you really like. Let's say you have a favorite baseball cap. You like wearing a baseball cap, so you decide to buy a few more caps with different designs. All of a sudden, you have a dozen or more baseball caps. Now these caps are scattered all over the place—and worse: You can't find your original cap—the one you prefer above all those others—because it's buried some-where in a pile.

Or decorative pillows. You tend not to associate pillows with clutter, and that's generally true. The general rule of thumb is two pillows for each head, with an allowance for one decorative pillow per head. But when the number of decorative pillows ticks past two per bed, the pillows have become another form of clutter. Your pillow collection has made getting ready for bed a chore, since you now have to put away half a dozen pillows every night.

Shoes. Here's where I'm likely to get into trouble with my female friends (and better-dressed male friends). I'm not go-ing to ask the question, "Do you really *need* all those shoes?" because shoe hoarders always claim they do, but I will pro-pose the possibility that owning such a wide variety of delight-ful shoes may make it less likely that you're going to enjoy your few favorite pairs of footwear. Why is that? I'm glad you asked. Let's say you have eight pairs of shoes, which, from my research, is the number of pairs of shoes in a starter collec-tion. (I happen to have two pairs, by way of reference.) Figur-ing out which shoe to wear may involve trying on each pair and examining them with your outfit: At 3½ minutes per pair times 8, that's 28 minutes, or close to half an hour. If, instead, you only have two pairs of shoes, that's 2 times 3½ or 7 min-utes. But wait, it's not even that, because when your two pairs are a pair of sneakers and a pair of dress shoes, all you have to do is ask yourself, "Am I getting dressed up for this occasion?" and that takes you only two seconds to determine. So there you are!

But there are other costs to having too many shoes besides what it does to your getting-ready-to-go-out time. There's the time spent getting the shoes in and out of their storage space.

There's the time spent keeping the shoes in top shoe shape. And then there's the occasional problem of "Where are the [fill-in-the-blank] shoes?" Because you have so many shoes, you may not be able to keep them in a single place, which can quickly lead to lost pairs. Now, let's say you tackle that problem by having a closet custom-built to organize and arrange your huge inventory of shoes. That's what Imelda Marcos did . . . and look what happened to her.*

Too many choices can actually limit your choices. Take, for example, those fun souvenir pens with the objects that float inside in a clear liquid in the barrel. We pick up one on nearly every trip we make. They're cute little reminders of the vacations we've had. My favorite pen is from Loch Ness, Scotland; it has a little monster floating through the lake. But after many years of traveling, we have lots of these pens. And you know what? They're not the best writing pens in the world. One or two is great, but now that we have nearly twenty, these decorative souvenir pens are crowding out the pens that actually do work.

Now for the solution. Lovers of multiple shoes and other possessions they consider essential are not going to like it, but here goes: Calculate the bare minimum number of the item you need to live a normal life, and get rid of the excess. True collectors of a rare or valuable type of thing: Build a museum or an archive to store your collection properly, so that it won't clutter up your house.

---

*She and her husband, dictator of the Philippines, were deposed from power, forced into exile, and her closets opened to display her wretched excess—3,000 pairs of shoes among them—to the gloating, revenge-driven people.

Defeat Clutter at Its Starting Point

When it comes to clutter, there's a right time to act, and there's too late. Have you ever finished up the last of the strawberry jam and rinsed out the jar but then been unable to decide whether to recycle it or use it as a kids' drinking glass or a pencil cup, so it just sat empty on your kitchen counter year after year? Have you ever gone through a box of old photos thinking you'd like to put them in chronological order, only to discover that you have no idea where and when most of them were taken? And what about all those little things, like pen tops and single mittens, that you can't put away properly because you're missing a part to make the item useful again?

As you look around your house, office, and car, you'll discover a zillion little things that wouldn't have become clutter if you had learned to deal with them the right way at the right time. I'm talking about empty CD cases, free bookmarks from Amazon.com, directions scribbled on the back of envelopes to a party you went to months ago and didn't like all that much anyway, unmatched socks (your dryer must have eaten the missing matches), keys to some door somewhere, miscellaneous receipts, eraser bits, fallen-off buttons, postcards from afar, party favors from your kid's last birthday bash, bubble wrap that might be reused, a great recipe torn from a magazine that you plan to try sometime (just not today), a membership renewal form, a stray computer disc—these are objects that you typically find "all over the place."

By itself a single one of these objects doesn't clutter up your house, but as a group of unrelated items, these stray objects are a primary cause of clutter. Throwing one pen cap away or putting one thing away—perhaps a sweater that's hanging over your staircase railing—won't affect the overall clutter quotient of your house, apartment, office, or car. But put a stop to the practice of leaving things out and you'll find the overall picture improving rapidly.

When all those little cluttering things are no longer building up, your perception of clutter will change. Clutter won't seem so omnipresent, so threatening. The little things are more than symbolic gestures; they're junkyard-dog-mean clutter (which is to say, they'll hang around forever and bite whenever they can). But you do have to *train* yourself to deal with them right away, or else they'll get the better of you. You do realize that they breed as soon as your back is turned. Pretty soon you're cluttered right out of your own home. (Just ask Imelda Marcos!)

OUTWITTING CLUTTER WARNING

At times outwitting clutter can be much, much harder than you ever imagined. A true story: A Washington, D.C., woman once donated a pair of her son's high school gym shorts to Goodwill. Years later the son found them for sale at a bazaar in Tanzania. It was fate saying, "Buy back these shorts."*

Walk and Carry

Walking from room to room? Take some clutter with you. Clutter has a way of migrating from the right place to the wrong place. Shoes end up in the family room; umbrellas end up in the car; briefcases in the living room; sunglasses in the kitchen; Scotch tape in the bathroom; the measuring tape in the basement . . . maybe you used it to figure out how to hem that pair of pants you hoped would shrink after you put them in the dryer, but they didn't. But how did that videotape case get into the

---

*If you don't believe this story, check it out yourself. It was reported by Kristin Lord in the October 18, 2001, issue of the *Washington Post*.

kitchen, where there's no VCR? Perhaps your spouse was reading the movie's description over the phone to someone. If you
can't remember how something got to be in the wrong place,
that object has been clutter for far too long. Still, with every trip
from room to room, you can undo this type of clutter, bit by bit.
After a week, you'll be amazed at the inroads you've made.

Before you leave a room, look around and think about
what's there but ought to be somewhere else. If you have kids—
or you're a child at heart—you're sure to keep an eye out for
tiny toys and games and puzzle pieces where they don't belong.
Often you'll find the stuff by stepping on it.

Never wasting a trip is a good trick to teach children, too. Often parents assign their kids the job of "cleaning up." But the
kids have absolutely no idea how to do that. (Many adults can't
figure it out either.) You need to give them very specific, step-by-
step instructions. If all you offer is a vague directive—"Put toys
in their proper place"—it's useless. To them, the best place for a
toy is out on the floor where it can be played with whenever they
happen to pass by. What you need to do at least once, and
maybe two or three times for a child under the age of seven, is
have the child watch you as you put each thing away exactly
where it's supposed to go.

Once the child can read, you can start labeling shelves and
bins: BOARD GAMES HERE. LEGOS ONLY. STUFFED ANIMALS LIVE HERE.

Some parents start doing this even before the child can read,
drawing pictures or using computer clip art to let the child see
which shelves and bins are for what types of toys or games.

Give Everyone Space

Everyone who lives with you needs his or her own "personal
space." This personal space isn't a place your spouse, roommate, children, or significant other can clutter up willy-nilly.

Rather it's a place that relates to a specific function. The personal space is rooted in the truth that everybody has different needs and has different roles in a household. For instance, my wife has a vanity table and I don't. She also has a cabinet that contains lotions and potions that go on the vanity. Now, if I owned that vanity, I would turn it into a desk, and if I had the cabinet, it would become a place where I could keep tools. But that's not the way things work in our house: Peggy owns that vanity outright and it's her space to do with as she sees fit.

Conversely, I have a drawer for computer parts, and my wife doesn't. Now and then Peggy covets that space, but it's mine—not to clutter as I want, but for the specific and silently negotiated purpose of storing computer parts.

Near our kitchen, which is the central nervous system in our house, is a shelf where all the school notes, programs, folders, and schedules are stored. Peggy is mostly responsible for keeping the school stuff in order, and so she gets to control that valuable real estate right next to the kitchen. Much as I would like that shelf for my video equipment, it's not mine according to the Treaty of House and Garage we have in place here.

Recognizing these different spaces is important to harmonious living. If two people are warring over the same territory, the potential for mutual annihilation will always be there. There are many common places in every house and apartment, but there are also very many individual spaces, too. You don't have to declare all these spaces in advance or map them. These personal spaces for particular purposes evolve over time.

If you are the owner of a designed personal space, you have an obligation to keep that space in some kind of order. Your ownership privileges may evaporate if you don't take care of the space you store your tools, cosmetics, CDs, or souvenir pens in. Your roommate, spouse, or even children may claim ownership over your territory if it becomes too cluttered. This is analogous to city zoning ordinances that give municipalities the right to confiscate property that isn't well maintained.

Indisputable Clutter: Stand Your Ground

Lots of us read cereal boxes during breakfast. It's almost an American tradition. While not the highest form of literature, cereal boxes can make for interesting time passers, especially before the coffee starts to work and our eyes can focus on the tiny print in the newspaper. There's nothing wrong with reading a cereal box at the breakfast table.

Are you wondering where this section is heading? I'll get to the point: While it's fine to read the back of the cereal box, and maybe even justified to save that box when it's empty to clip out the contest coupon and mail it in with the hope of winning a million dollars, it's *not* fine to leave the empty box lying around for the next six months. It's not literature. It's not an art object. It's not even a potential art object (because I'm telling you now, even if your child's school asks you to save cereal boxes to send in to be turned into a diorama, you're better off grabbing a half-full box, emptying the uneaten cereal into a Tupperware container, and then sending in the freshly empty carton, than you are hanging on to old cereal boxes, just for that event). Saving a cereal box is *always wrong*. Empty cereal boxes are always clutter. There are no ifs about it. If you can't throw out your old cereal boxes after you finish the cereal within, you will never be able to defeat clutter. And if you live with a person who insists on saving empty cereal boxes, you must put your foot down. Say: "It's clutter, and it goes!" And let that be the end of it.

That was an easy case. Now let's try one a bit more controversial: a box of trash bags. Trash bags are supposed to be one of the tools we use to conquer clutter. But if one day a member of your household sees an industrial-sized box of trash bags on sale—*300 on a roll! Less than five cents a bag!*—and can't resist buying ten boxes at that price, but your house lacks a suitable storage place to keep all these extra boxes of trash bags, they'll turn into clutter. They will sit in a tall stack by your back door, obstructing your entry and exit, until you take action. What to do with them? Figure out how many bags you use in a year (approximately) and keep that number in your usual storage space; the rest you should give away to any organization that performs disaster cleanup after hurricanes or tornadoes (like the Red Cross). Trash bags are always needed. Don't forget to get a receipt for the donation and put it immediately in your "Charitable Donations" file.

With me so far? Now let's move on to a slightly more difficult case: The flowers that arrived in honor of your anniversary came in a lovely vase. Once the flowers started to wilt, you had no trouble tossing them, did you? What about the vase still sitting on your kitchen counter—is that indisputably clutter? After all, it's reusable. But think—every time you're sent a fancy arrangement, *it comes in a vase.* How often does someone give you cut flowers that you must put in a vase yourself? And don't you already have two or three vases for just such an occasion? How many vases do you need, anyway? Convinced? If so, all you need to do now is figure out the best way to dispose of an extra vase. The simplest thing to do is to throw it out. That's right. Toss it, without a second thought. Otherwise, you'll find yourself pondering the appropriateness of an empty vase as a gift for this or that person, and then having to set up an opportunity for that person to receive the gift and take it away. All the while the empty vase sits on your counter, cluttering it up. But act quickly, boldly, and decisively, and you keep your enemy, clutter, at bay. What about foisting clutter on someone else.

Every time you go to someone's house for dinner, bring them fresh cut flowers in a vase.

Battles and warfare, while I'm on that subject, are a good, ongoing metaphor to help you achieve your goal. You must never let down your guard. Don't let clutter sneak up on you. Clutter is clever—it will often disguise itself as something benign. Look upon gifts, and extra vases, and bargain boxes of trash bags and other super-sized products as what they truly are: Trojan Clutter Horses. And then aggressively, even ruthlessly, defend your home against them!

Decluttering for Profit

Outwitting clutter is *not* throwing everything away.

Some things are simply too valuable to toss. Even if an item isn't worth a lot of money, it's still hard for most of us to throw away something we know still works, and that someone else might find useful. It just seems wrong to be so wasteful. Besides that, most of us could really use the money. It's great when you're able to combine two worthwhile pursuits in one project, outwitting clutter and making some extra money at the same time.

On the other hand, the notion that "It would be a waste of money just to throw this away" all too often serves as a smokescreen for inaction. Instead, let it serve as a spur to find and put into reality that alternate, nonwasteful means of dealing with the object.

These alternatives include:

- Charitable giveaways (to Goodwill, the Salvation Army, or other organizations that resell household goods), providing you with a receipt that reduces your tax burden at the end of the year.

- Advertising and selling the individual item (through a posted notice, a flyer, or a newspaper ad).
- Offering the individual item for online auction (through eBay or some other effective online sales outlet).
- Selling the item along with a lot of other things in a yard sale or garage sale that you put on.
- Selling the item along with a lot of other things in a sale organized by your block, community group, or other social organization.

There are pluses and minuses to each of these courses of action, and I'll mention a few of them for each, in the same order as above.

Donating to charity. On the plus side, you can get rid of the stuff quickly and you know that the money will go to a good cause. Most charities accept donations all year round. Some charities will even pick up for you. On the minus side, you don't get paid, you merely get some tax relief at the end of the year. If you don't itemize your taxes, that may not be enough incentive to get you going.

Selling the item on your own through ads. On the plus side, you get all the money from the sale, after you've subtracted the cost of the ad. If you use a community bulletin board, your ad may just be an index card with the sales information on it and will cost you nothing. You can sell when it's convenient to you, screening potential customers over the phone and setting up appointments with likely buyers. On the minus side, there's a variable amount of hassle involved in preparing an ad and arranging appointments to show the item to buyers.

Selling the item online. On the plus side, online auctions are very effective at matching people who want junk with the people who want to unload it. The cost of selling through eBay, for example, is minimal, and the buyer pays for shipping. On the minus side—and take this for the very strong caution that it is—eBay can be addictive! Once you start browsing through categories with the idea of finding the right place to post your offering, you could very well come across stuff you want to buy. If you yield to temptation, all advantage is lost, and you end up spending money to acquire clutter, rather than the desired, opposite result.

Holding a yard or garage sale. The big plus is that you get rid of a lot of clutter at once. You don't have to make appointments with lots of individual buyers—you just advertise the sale on flyers around the neighborhood, and maybe in a small, cheap ad in a neighborhood newspaper, and wait for buyers to show up within your announced time frame. You get paid cash on the spot, and the people haul your stuff away. The big minus is that it takes a fair amount of time and effort to organize a yard sale, or at least to do it well. There are how-to books dedicated to this subject alone. You have to lay all the stuff out, be there during the stated hours, and, worst of all, listen to strangers traipse around picking up your once treasured things, muttering loudly enough for you to hear, "Bleah, this is the ugliest lamp I've ever seen! Who would ever want *this*?"

Participating in a group yard sale. On the plus side, you split up the duties among your neighbors or other group participants. You do more advertising and have more to offer, thus attracting more buyers. On the minus side, you can't schedule the sale whenever you want; it must be a group decision. Your items are in competition with your neighbors' things in attracting the attention of buyers. And you're still stuck there while strangers pick through your things and make insultingly low offers.

How about this for a creative twist on the yard-sale idea? You give your salable clutter to a friend who's planning a yard sale. Your friend makes all the arrangements for the sale ahead of time, is there for the bargaining and the cash handling, and deals with any unsold items afterward—but your friend also gets to keep the lion's share of the proceeds. You settle for, say, 25 or 30 percent. (If you drive a hard bargain and have some really good stuff for the sale, then try to get 40 or even 50 or more percent.) That sounds to me like a win–win situation!

Get Some Giveaway Friends

There are times when you don't have enough clutter to give away in organized batches. You've just got one thing—say, an extra desk lamp. You know you can't sell it for much because the base is cracked. For these occasions it's useful to have a circle of friends or acquaintances who like or need all kinds of stuff. These don't have to be good friends, just people who are interested in what you're no longer interested in. You could find somebody who just wants books and somebody else who just wants kids' clothing. Best of all would be to find somebody who likes *everything*. Newlyweds or the newly divorced are usually good. College students, even better. It doesn't matter—as long as you have somebody who can take away your stuff.

How do you find such a person? Well, it's likely that you already know somebody who thrives on clutter, but you just don't know who that person is. Rather than asking everyone you know, "Do you want my old junk?" a more discreet question would be, "I have a lot of things I no longer need, such as old records, shoes, cooking utensils. From time to time I go through my house and collect some stuff to give away. Interested in being on my call list?" If your acquaintance says, "Sure, I'd love to get a lot of stuff for free," ask no more questions. Most importantly, don't worry about whether the person can really use the stuff or is going to turn around and sell it, or give it away to somebody else. Motive doesn't matter as much as the practical effect: You've got somebody to dump stuff on, and beyond lifting the receiver and dialing the telephone, you don't have to do a thing. You now have a symbiotic relationship, and all that matters is that it works.

Is it ethical to pawn your clutter off on somebody else? Can you morally justify this kind of behavior? Yes. It's moral and right and ethical and even beneficial. Just because the only way you can think of to get rid of clutter is to give it away doesn't mean that's the clutter's ultimate fate. Don't feel bad about foisting your junk off on somebody else. That somebody might be making a thousand a year selling your former clutter. If that turns out to be the case, don't feel you've been taken advantage of, either. That person did the work of advertising the stuff, screening the potential buyers, setting up appointments (and half the time the person doesn't show up), and bargaining over the worth of the thing. That's a lot of work that you didn't want to do. It's only fair that the person who does the work reaps the profit.

The Ten Pillars of Uncluttered Wisdom

I.   Establish the principle that every piece of furniture must serve its own specific purpose and no other. For example, chairs are not magazine racks. The kitchen table is not the place to store your kids' art projects. Couches are not bookshelves.

II. Visualize your house empty. It's all too easy to accept clutter as ordinary, part of the way things should be. But if you start to think of your house the way it was before you moved in, you'll have an easier time recognizing and removing that which is excess.

III.   The moment you start to put something in a place in the wrong way, stop and ask yourself, "How can I put this right?" Then do so.

IV.   Don't ignore, procrastinate, or rationalize your clutter away. Keep your mind focused on your goal and your path will remain uncluttered and your movements free and confident.

V.   Don't envy your friends for having material things you lack. Don't *ever* buy something because "everyone's" got one, or you will surely end your days wallowing in nothing but clutter.

VI.   Don't throw out the clutter of another without receiving permission. To do so is a form of stealing. On the other hand, don't worry too much about what constitutes permission. A mumbled "uh-huh" or a nod of a sleepy head is still a yes.

VII. Be aware of the passage of time. Do not waste opportunities to declutter when you have the time. Recognize that a well-organized life means more time for you to do better things.

VIII. Keep things that have sentimental value, but also keep in mind that not everything that has *ever* held sentimental value needs to be saved. In other words, one or two souvenirs from each vacation or romantic relationship should be enough.

IX.   Accept that you are human and imperfect and can never live a completely clutter-free life. Learn to love the clutter you can't remove and tolerate that which can only be removed at too great a cost.

X.   Your things are just that—things. They are not humans and certainly not gods. Do not let them rule your life.

3

Clutter Around the House

Back to the Uncluttered Past?

Remember when you first looked at your house or apartment? Before you moved in, your home was in pristine condition, spacious, airy, and welcoming. It had possibilities—possibilities that gave you a sense of endless freedom and creativity and self-expression.

Then what did you do? You cluttered the place up. Why did you make such a mess?

The answer is simply that life involves clutter. There's no way to avoid clutter completely; nor should you even try. If you want to live in your new apartment on just a sleeping bag with nothing else around, go ahead: That would certainly make your place clutter-free, but it would be a boring, unfriendly arrangement. Who wants to live that way?

Whether you invite clutter into your house or clutter barges in unannounced, you're going to have stuff that needs to be tended to. This chapter outlines the steps you can take to tame the clutter so that it doesn't take over and interfere with your ability to find things when you need them and get done what you need to do. You will *not* learn how to create a sterile environment, a place so clean you could perform open-heart surgery in it.

Also, keep in mind—as ever—that I offer guidelines only; everybody's environment is different, so you have to be willing to adapt.

The Stairs (and Other High-Priority Parts of the House)

Nothing ever belongs on the stairs. Stairs are not a storage area. This isn't just a matter of aesthetics; it's an essential safety concern, too. You can easily trip on any object on the stairs. And if you think that you'll see what's on the stairs, avoid it, and not slip, well, maybe that's true. (But I doubt it's true at night.) Can you make the same promise, however, about your klutzy spouse and your little children? One mother reported, "Today I have to clean the clutter out of the stairs and hallway. One of my kids got tangled up and slipped down about four stairs." That was the incentive she needed; fortunately, the spill was a minor one.

Clutter anywhere on the floor, in fact, only invites accidents. Whenever there's something on a floor besides the floor itself, the odds are that somebody sometime is going to slip or stumble over that something. If it's simply a loose piece of paper and you just slide a bit when you step on it, then no harm done. But if it's a Matchbox car and it sends you careening headfirst into a sliding glass door, then you're probably talking about a visit to the emergency room.

Make removing potentially dangerous clutter your first priority. What else falls into the category of dangerous clutter? Clutter in front of space heaters. Clutter on top of heaters! In our house we have a oil-filled space heater in the family room because it's the draftiest room in our drafty old house. We also have some throw blankets in the family room: It feels cozy to

A big no-no!

snuggle under a blanket while you're playing Monopoly on a cold winter's evening.

The problem is what to do with the blankets and the space heater in the spring when both these warm-up measures are unnecessary. The first summer after we'd finished using the space heater for the season, we unplugged it and pushed it back behind an end table, and then folded up the blankets and laid them on top of the heater. There they sat all summer long. In the fall, out came the blankets again. The space heater got plugged back in and moved forward again. Then one evening after the kids had finished playing a board game, I came into the family room to find the game pieces put neatly away and the blankets neatly folded, too . . . and placed right on top of the (very hot) space heater. Well, that's just where the kids assumed they went, having seen them there all summer. And they were so proud of themselves for having straightened up!

At once I changed the system. I established a place for the folded blankets in the opposite corner from the space heater. And the minute after the space heater gets unplugged in the spring, it goes right downstairs to the basement for storage until the next fall. The blankets, too, go into blanket storage, sealed inside mothproof zippered plastic bags and tucked away in our cedar-lined closet until the cold weather returns. I now have these things on a seasonal to-do list, along with changing the clocks for Daylight Saving Time twice a year.

Other dangerous things that shouldn't be treated as ordinary clutter include:

- Flammable things, such as gasoline, oils, kerosene, and rubbing alcohol. Keep well away from sources of heat or flame.
- Toxic materials, including pesticides, fungicides, and petroleum-based cleaning supplies—all these need to be put

in a safe, dry, protected place, completely inaccessible to children or pets. Even if you have no children or pets, don't leave poisons out, because you can't account for unexpected visitors.

- Sharp objects, especially knives, have to be put away in their proper places. If you use a box cutter to open your packages, put it away after each use without delay. Remember, any type of uncovered blade can come back to bite you. Straight pins and sewing needles left on the couch or floor are more than just clutter—they're tiny flesh-seeking missiles trying to embed themselves in some human pincushion. You are warned!

- Extension cords. Yikes! Electric extension cords are the essence of clutter. People can trip over them. They can cause fires. (Did you know that extension cords have maximum amp ratings? You can't use a conventional extension cord with certain high-power equipment, such as air conditioners and electric lawn mowers.) If you follow the trail of an extension cord and it leads nowhere, you've found an accident waiting to happen. Coil it up and store it away until you actually have a use for it.

Temporary Clutter

Perhaps the most insidious, sticky, hard-to-get-rid-of type of house clutter is what I call "temporary clutter."

Temporary clutter is the stuff that we put in our front halls, dining rooms, bedroom floors, kitchen counters, and elsewhere—"just temporarily"—because we need those things for a school project, sign making for our church, synagogue, or mosque's flea market, Halloween costume making, income tax preparation, toaster repair, photo album organizing, and other activities.

Temporary clutter can take up a lot of space. I know, because last Halloween the costume making seemed to take over my whole house. Well, that's an exaggeration, but certainly the dining room table was completely covered up with the fabric and trimmings to make a turkey suit, complete with a beak, wings, huge tail, and lots of stuffing (for our ten-year-old) and the cardboard and stick-on numbers to create a silver-and-gold clock with movable hands (our seven-year-old). For several weeks before the big day our family was forced to eat out far more than was healthy for us at our local McDonald's (leaving us with the concomitant problem of what to do with all those Happy Meal toys we accumulate—but that's for another chapter). When you're in the throes of some "short-term" project, the floor space of an entire room can be turned into a "Don't Walk" zone. One or the other parent can even be prohibited from taking a nap on a bed that's been transformed into a fabric layout table.

Still worse: We are *all* guilty of this at one time or another. Who among us hasn't taken over a space to work on taxes, prepare birthday party loot bags, or sort clothes to be given away into various piles? (The "give away" pile may disappear quickly, and so may the "okay to keep and wear" pile; it's the "not okay to give away but not okay to wear, either" pile that never seems to budge once it's been created.) Then there's the everyday pileup of mail left on the hall table that falls into the category of "I'll look at it later." As a writer, I'm familiar with the newspaper category of temporary clutter occurring when I leave a note on an article saying "Save for me—may be useful for the book I'm working on." Whether I've actually ever gone back and used a piece of information from any of these newspaper articles that were saved at my insistence is open to question. I have no doubt I've kept my wife from throwing out ad circulars from different electronics stores because I was sure I was going to do some price comparisons before buying, and then went right out and bought the first thing I saw. Yes, to this one I must plead guilty (couldn't deny it, since I've been caught red-handed more than once).

But leaving aside which spouse creates more temporary clutter than the other, the question remains: How do you deal with this so-called temporary clutter? While it's hard to set a precise method because temporary clutter takes many guises (or should I say *disguises*?), I have come up with some general techniques you can use.

The first is: Whenever you're about to start a temporary clutter pile, be it a newspaper that's waiting to be clipped or a sewing project you have yet to start, set a firm time limit for that clutter. And stick to that cutoff date. This is a minimum and a must. When you reach your deadline, either finish the project, throw it out, or abandon the idea entirely. Make sure everyone knows the cutoff date, too, so your family members aren't wondering when you're going to abandon your slob ways—they'll have an answer to the question they thought was rhetorical. If it helps, mark that glorious date on your calendar, sign a contract, or put a Post-it note on the stuff. But whatever else you do, it's essential that the target date not be ignored or extended.

Oh, and by the way: The shorter the time frame you set, the better. That means at both ends. You want to end the temporary clutter project as soon as you can, but you also want to delay its start for as long as possible. Why begin to assemble your child's birthday party loot bags as soon as you get the bags? Instead, you can put the bags and the candy and toys in the closet until the day before the party. Do you really need to assemble all your tools to repair your son's bicycle today (Monday) when he's not going cycling until Saturday, and you're not actually going to get around to the project until Friday after work? Can you wait to triage your dresser drawers until a time that's closer to your congregation's annual fall clothing-for-the-homeless drive?

What else can you do to help alleviate the symptoms of temporary clutter? Ask yourself: "Do I really need all that space to do this project? Do I need the entire kitchen counter, family room couch, or front porch to do what I'm doing? Or is part of that space sufficient?" If there's any possibility of using part of a room or surface, just commandeer what you need. When the government needs to take over land to build a highway, does it use the power of eminent domain to control the entire town in which the highway will be situated, or just the strip of land that is needed?

Borrow a page—or an aisle—from department and drugstores. Create a seasonal place in your house for all those temporary projects, many of which are related to specific holidays. Stores often have an entire area or aisle that changes goods depending on the season. Almost everything in the store remains the same throughout the year, but the products in this particular section change. Do the same thing at home.

That seasonal place could be a long table in your basement or a corner of your family room—whatever works for your situation. And don't just reserve that space for temporary clutter: Use it year-round, but make sure that everyone in your household is aware that this space may be taken over now by the temporary project.

Conversely, if you set up this system, you must—absolutely must—not use any other part of your house or apartment for projects that cause an undue amount of clutter. It's only fair.

Some temporary clutter may not lend itself to a particular place or even take up that much room, but it may be clutter nonetheless. Next year's calendar, purchased four months early, is one example.

Because not every clutter problem has a predefined solution, you'll have to improvise. The calendar is something you're going to use, just not now. If, in September, you put the calendar in a "safe place," come December you may have no idea where that safe place is. So put the calendar partly out of the way, but in a place that you'll either remember or see regularly. The logical place is hanging on a hook behind this year's calendar. If you're talking about the desktop variety, then leave it in its box in a drawer you use every day. I put my next-year's calendar in my shirt drawer, where it takes up little room and I see it every time I put on a clean shirt.

Clutter on the Way to Class

Dear Clutter Adviser:

I'm taking a photography course—I'm thinking of changing careers and becoming a professional photographer. I subscribe to several photography magazines and newsletters. I don't need to keep these magazines after I'm done with them, so I bring them to the class to give to the other students. The problem is that the class only meets once every two weeks, so I often have a pile of read magazines sitting around for a week or more. What can I do to put a stop to this temporary clutter?

Sincerely,

Shutterbug

Dear Shutterbug,

You get a lot of points for giving away the magazines in the first place. Many people would keep them for years and years, thereby contributing to the downfall of civilization. The path of least resistance is to leave the magazines you plan to give away in a pile on your downstairs front hall table. And it's the path of least resistance that often leads directly to hell. So, good for you.

To achieve a higher plane of outwitting clutter, you should do something like put the read magazines in your camera bag right after you've finished them. If your camera bag isn't big enough, put them in a plastic shopping bag and hang the bag on the *inside* doorknob of your front hall closet. The bag is strategically invisible, and, if you're true to your desires, you'll empty that bag every other week.

The Backs of Doors

Space is a precious resource. Space has *everything* to do with clutter, because if we had an infinite amount of space, we might have an infinite amount of clutter, too, but at least all that clutter would have someplace to go.

Children's rooms pose a special challenge, because they need all the pieces of furniture that adults need (bed, dresser, desk, chair) plus shelves or bins for their toys, but their rooms are usually smaller than the adults' bedroom. One idea that we've put to good use in our kids' rooms, as well as elsewhere in the house, is to make use of space that would otherwise be wasted. I'm talking about the vertical surfaces of doors. At many a hardware, home improvement, organizing, and children's store you can purchase over-the-door hangers with hooks, shelves, or shoe pockets. With a little creativity, you can use the space behind the door to hold just about anything—books, toys, diaper supplies, bathrobes and pajamas, the laundry bag, shoes, a mirror and grooming products. Over-the-door bags and shelves are at just the right height for kids to reach, so your children can become involved in putting things away there. Both boys and girls like the idea of trying to toss their dirty clothes into a laundry bag that's set up like a basketball hoop with the door as the backstop. There's certainly nothing wrong with making cleanup time fun.

The Safe-Place Problem

"I'll put this in a safe place," you say to yourself. That's one way to deal with certain kinds of clutter. But you also know when you do this that chances are fifty-fifty that by the time you need to retrieve the item, you'll have no idea where its safe place happens to be. No idea whatsoever.

Still, the safe-place concept is a good one. The safe-place technique usually tames clutter, because safe places are mostly out of the way and uncluttered. Things put in a safe place usually aren't in the way of anything else and don't interfere with your day-to-day activities.

But how in the world do you remember where the safe place is? That's easy. You keep a list. Right there in your address book, or electronic address book, create an entry under *S* for "safe place." Even if you forget that you've put the information in your address book—something that's quite possible—there's a good chance that you'll happen upon that safe-place entry when looking through your address book for something else.

Many people put a note on their bulletin board, or use a Post-it note, for things in their safe places. That's a bad idea. Bulletin boards become quickly cluttered, and Post-it notes get lost. (Remember, the adhesive on the back of Post-it notes is *designed* to be only very slightly sticky, so that it can be removed without leaving a trace.)

You're welcome to design your own method, but it should include putting the whereabouts in a permanent, findable location.

If you decide to use your address book to solve the safe-place problem, you'll discover that it can also be used to help outwit clutter on a number of fronts. You can put the location of your will in your address book under *W*. You can put your driver's license number, passport number, kid's school locker number and combination, Internet provider password—everything you may need to know—in your address book. You'll really make a dent in a great variety of types of clutter by using your address book for a wide range of nontraditional purposes. As I mentioned, the beauty of putting all this information in your address book is that it's something you're unlikely to misplace or lose.

Into your address book should also go important family records, such as safe deposit box numbers and bank account information. (To be on the safe side, never store your PIN in the same place as the account number.) If something tragic happens to you, it's probable that somebody will eventually find and consult your address book. If you keep an electronic address book, consider printing a copy from time to time and putting that copy in your filing cabinet (you have a filing system, right?) under "Address Book." (Because an electronic address book is so useful in helping reduce digital clutter, you'll find much more on this subject in the "Office Clutter" chapter.) Your ordinary address book is one of the most potent anticlutter tools you have. Use it regularly, and use it creatively.

Room Decluttering: Two Strategies—Whole Hog or Piecemeal

When you are thoroughly fed up with the clutter in a particular part of your house, draw up a plan to go through everything and decide what to do with it, whether to keep it or toss it—and if you keep it, where it gets put back.

Here's what's involved in doing the average bedroom in an average house:

- Go through all things on the shelves, shelf by shelf.
- Go through all drawers, one drawer at a time.
- Go through all items piled on top of flat surfaces.
- Go through any other types of containers found in the room (including jewelry boxes and change jars).
- Unplug devices and untangle power cords.
- Inspect all pictures in frames on dresser tops and hung on walls and decide if you want to keep these snapshots.
- Open up the closet(s) and inventory the contents.
- Go through everything on the floor.
- Deal with any items not in any of these places (for example, on windowsills, hooks, and under the bed).

You may want to approach your room in either the "whole hog" fashion or the "piecemeal" fashion. When you go whole hog, you'll be taking everything out of drawers and off shelves and out of containers, but not beginning the triage process until you've moved everything from its resting place. Then you look at everything to be put back with a critical eye. If you can add it to the get-rid-of pile, you're spared from having to put it back—meaning less work for you. It's a lot easier and faster to throw out or give away one huge pile of stuff than it is to make lots and lots of little piles (as will be the case if you take the piecemeal approach, described below).

The main problem with the whole hog approach is that you'll need to devote a large block of time to doing the whole room at once, or else you'll leave the room half done, with far more mess on the floor waiting to be triaged than a normal person could live with. But this is the way to go if you want to force yourself to do the whole room in one day.

If you want to go at it shelf by shelf, drawer by drawer, in small increments over a long period of time, then the piecemeal method is the right way to proceed. You do the same thing as in the whole hog method: Take everything down, inspect, evaluate, and triage (that is, decide how each thing is to be handled, whether it is to be put back in its original place, moved to another place, given away, sold, or thrown out). You just perform all these actions for one small piece of the room, let's say a bookshelf, before moving on to the next piece, such as the top dresser drawer.

You don't have to do the whole room in a day to have a livable space. You can probably do a small dresser in less than an hour, a large set of bookshelves in an hour or two, and have the things back in their place neatly, inspiring you to move on to the next part of the room as soon as you have another hour to spare.

The whole hog method is something best done by a couple working together. The piecemeal method can easily be broken into individual assignments: For example, she does the dresser drawers holding her own clothes; he sticks to the ones that hold his—although both have pledged to get rid of at least two shopping bagfuls each.

Note that large, extremely cluttered spaces may require a full family effort. Basements, garages, and attics can easily be weekend or even multiweekend jobs. You may need to set down some ground rules for all the members of the team. (See the sidebar for some sample ground rules.)

One trick you may find helpful is to pretend that you're moving out of a particular room. Tell yourself the prospective buyer needs to see it in its best light. It must look pristine. Nothing can be left "for later." Arrange for somebody else to look at it when you think you're done and tell you what still looks messy or out of place. It helps if that outside observer is a real estate agent or interior designer or architect—someone with a trained eye for the appearance and value of space.

Here's yet another mental exercise: Imagine that you drop dead with the room exactly as it is, cluttered. Now think about your children or grandchildren or some other heirs (greedy distant cousins, perhaps?) coming to clean out your stuff. Is there anything you wouldn't want them to find? Old gum wrappers that missed the wastebasket, certainly, but what about that pack of cigarettes stashed at the back of the desk drawer that you hung on to after you quit smoking more than a decade ago, "just in case"? And do you really want anyone to suspect that you ever *wore* that tie-dye shirt with the slogan spelled out in Day-Glo paint, ACID IS GROOVY?

This sort of self-questioning can get you to recognize problems that you otherwise might have rationalized away. But if you don't find this approach productive, be creative and come up with your own means of making yourself part with excess stuff. Once you find a way that helps you make inroads, you'll find yourself improving upon it, embellishing it, making it

Ground Rules for Room Decluttering

- Nothing found will be regarded as sacrosanct (or, conversely: Everything related to Mom's days as star of the college track team shall be regarded as sacrosanct and left undisturbed).
- Everything shall be inspected. Every box will be opened, every piece of furniture looked behind, every closet emptied out completely.
- No duplicates permitted. That is to say, just because Dad bought his copy of *Dark Side of the Moon* with the money from his first job and Mom got hers as a present from her first real boyfriend, that doesn't mean you should keep both. One of them still has to go.
- Nothing will go back into a temporary space. That is, if you lack shelf space for all the books you've decided to keep, you're not done until you either (1) think harder about what to get rid of, until you're down to the exact number that will fit on the shelves, or (2) come up with additional, permanent bookshelf space. Stacking books on top of other books or in piles on top of the shelf in a way that makes them look like clutter is unacceptable.
- You're not done until all members of the decluttering team agree that you're done. If one person still thinks there is a clutter problem in the room, keep at it until you solve the remaining problem.
- Don't stop to eat until you're done (unless of course it's a daylong or multiday-long project). But when you are done, be sure to reward yourself with a victory feast of chocolate cake or whatever sort of food you reserve for special occasions.

work ever more efficiently. Then you take your new, improved decluttering approach and apply it with even greater fervor to the next room, and the next, until finally your whole house is clutter-free.

OUTWITTING CLUTTER TIP

We are what we leave behind. Strive to live so that you don't leave a mess for your kids.

Decluttering by Theme

Instead of tackling your house clutter room by room, tackle the problem by theme. While the strategies discussed earlier involve decluttering by location, you might be able to combat it more efficiently by taking a category approach.

Let's say you have a desk drawer that's all cluttered up. In that drawer are batteries, pens, paper clips, rubber bands, pepper spray, an expired library card, reservation confirmations for a forthcoming trip, your Swiss Army knife, a watch, assorted coins and bills, a few tie clips, a Palm Pilot case, exposed film that needs to be taken in for processing, a letter from the IRS you'd rather not have to read, your AAA membership card, a picture of an ex-girlfriend (make a note to move to a more secure location), a working calculator, a broken calculator, a couple of dull-pointed pencils but no sharpener, a small FM radio that may or may not work, and a few other odds and ends. This is clearly a drawer that's begging to be decluttered. But to declutter this drawer as a location, you have to be prepared to move dozens of different items to dozens of other locations (and throw stuff out, of course). What can make uncluttering by location so daunting is the challenge of figuring out where else everything should go (kind of like doing a jigsaw puzzle without the final picture in front of you), and then physically moving this thing to one place and that thing to another and a third thing to some other place entirely, and then returning to the original location, in this case, the drawer. Worst of all, after you've done all that, you find you still have a lot more to do, and you're not any farther along with that one stubborn problem of where to put that photo of you getting kissed on the mouth by Cindy after you won the high jump now that you're married to Cindy's younger sister Sue.

So you quit, with the drawer only half done. Incomplete de-cluttering may feel as bad as never having started in the first place, because you may think to yourself, "I've put all this effort and time into emptying the drawer, but it's still a mess."

If this has happened to you, I say try a different approach to dealing with a difficult cluttered space: Forget about the drawer. Leave undisturbed those items of clutter that you simply are unable or unwilling to classify and move. Focus instead on those items that easily fit into workable categories of clutter: organize by theme. For example: Just organize *all the batteries* in your house. (Please note that *all* was included in the italicized phrase.) First figure out a place where all your batteries can go. (Here's one idea: You can buy battery organizers that hang on the inside of closet doors and that come with battery testers. Or you could set aside a specific battery drawer. I know of a guy who keeps his batteries in a small shopping bag that hangs from the inside of a closet door (but his wife keeps threatening to move it to the inside of his workroom door). It doesn't really matter where your battery place is, as long as it meets a couple of criteria: The place should be reserved for batteries only, and it should be accessible. A battery place that's at the bottom of your linen closet, for example, is a bad idea.

Once you have the battery place set up, go around your house just gathering batteries. D's, C's, 9-volts, As, AAs, AAAs, AAAAs, even button batteries should go in the battery place. Take a battery tester along on this house-walk so that you can toss any expired batteries. The beauty of outwitting clutter thematically rather than geographically—that is, room by room—is that it doesn't matter so much if the particular theme is incomplete. If a day or a week later you find another battery someplace, you can easily add it to the battery place you've created.

The downside to using the thematic approach is that it can take longer to outwit clutter than if you go full force and attack a particular room. But you are less likely to experience that emotional letdown that can accompany an incomplete decluttering.

You can use the thematic approach to a wide variety of kinds of clutter. Here are some possible targets for this method:

- Baseball caps.
- Sports equipment (especially for specific sports).
- Car supplies.
- Computer accessories.
- Hairbrushes and hair accessories.
- Cosmetics.
- Medications, vitamins, and supplements.
- Postage stamps and mailing supplies.
- Restaurant delivery menus.
- Key rings (how many do you need, anyway?) and keys.
- Cell phones and chargers, other cell phone accessories, and spare cell phone batteries.
- Lightbulbs.
- Boots (if you visited our house, you'd understand why that's on the list).

Of course, there are plenty of things that need to be kept in multiple locations, such as scissors, lip balm, and fire extinguishers, but many other things, such as laser printer paper—and boots—that really do belong only in one place. Take a look at your house from a thematic perspective and figure out which items are good to disperse, and which should be centralized.

Undone by Unpacking

Dear Clutter Adviser:

After a trip, it takes forever for me to unpack. My suitcase sits around and nothing gets done with what's in it. What can I do to keep my suitcase from cluttering up my small apartment after a trip?

Signed,

Happy to Be Home

Dear H2BH,

You are suffering from Post-Traumatic Travel Stress Syndrome. Otherwise known as laziness.

In short, what you need to do is get off your behind and start unpacking.

However, you should consider the most likely reason why you're slow to start unpacking, and that's because your suitcase contains a wide variety of items. If all you had inside were dirty clothes, it would be a simple matter of just putting everything in the washer. But because there's a mix of dirty clothes, clean clothes, souvenirs, receipts, foreign money, domestic money, postcards, batteries, film, assorted documents, airplane tickets, shoes, coats, gadgets, and more, it's a daunting task to unpack: Unpacking means multiple trips to different places in your apartment. The coat goes in the front hall closet, the camera in a desk drawer, the film to be sent off for processing, the used airplane tickets you need in case you weren't credited the frequent flier points you are due, and so on. Outwitting clutter is a fairly easy task if it just involves a walk from point A to point B. But when outwitting clutter involves walking from point A to point B, then back to A, then from A to C, back to A, from A to D, back to A . . . well, that's a different matter.

So rather than suffer from inertia, break the unpacking down into discrete assignments. Put away the clean clothes first. Next, do the dirty clothes wash. Then when you're ready, take care of the film. Followed by the souvenirs. Set yourself an easy-to-follow, even leisurely schedule of what unpacking you will do on which day of the week, kind of like your itinerary from the trip you took: If it's Tuesday, it must be wash day. But never let the unpacking take longer than the original trip.

Another approach is to limit the amount and type of things you put in your suitcase to begin with. Unpacking is a lot faster and easier when all you have to do is put away the barest of essentials. Get a reliable weather report and pack only for the expected forecast. (If you need more warmth, you can always wear multiple layers of the clothing you brought—or buy an extra sweater during the trip, if you must.) Consider disposable things, too. Instead of packing a bulky raincoat, toss in a disposable plastic poncho. Find out whether the place where you'll be staying has a hair dryer and a bathrobe and you don't have to bring your own. And don't bring back anything you realize has been ruined during the trip. Those hiking boots that you discovered fit badly and gave you blisters can't be fixed—so leave them for one of the workers at the mountain lodge, who may find a good home for them. Your suitcase will thank you for everything you do that lightens its load.

OUTWITTING CLUTTER TIP

Get a battery tester. With it you'll be able to tell which batteries have life left in them, and which are C-L-U-T-T-E-R.

The Kitchen: Its Most Common Clutter Problems Attacked

As a clutter expert, I've spent time (way too much time!) listening to people complain about their clutter problems. When it comes to kitchens, I've learned that the complaints tend to fall under one of three rubrics:

1. The kitchen is a magnet for clutter (that is, every type of thing ends up there, whether it belongs there or not).
2. Pots and pans overflow their cabinets.
3. The refrigerator is a clutter nightmare unto itself.

I'll take these on one by one.

The kitchen as clutter magnet. The kitchen ends up being a storage place for many things that have absolutely nothing to do with food. That may be because kitchens are often the central meeting place in homes—kind of the town hall, if you will. I'm willing to bet that in your kitchen are things you hardly ever use, or haven't ever used, some of which don't even involve cooking. Let's start with phone books. How many do you have? Your residential directory, the Yellow Pages, perhaps a competing business directory put out by another phone company. Directories from neighboring counties. Directories from associations and schools. And then there are all the outdated directories that you still have on hand, waiting for a recycling pickup date that never seems to be announced. You don't need all these books, and the ones you keep can go someplace else. If your kitchen is indeed the site of the most frequently used phone in the house, then perhaps leave the most frequently consulted directory nearby. Put the others on a bookshelf with your other reference books, and be sure to get rid of last year's book the day the new one arrives.

Speaking of books, how many cookbooks do you own? And why are they all in the kitchen? If you have fifteen but have only ever consulted three of them, put the others in a place where there's more room (like, say, the collection bin for your school's rummage sale). At approximately one inch per book, you've instantly created a foot of extra shelf space in your kitchen.

What else is in your kitchen that doesn't belong? Many people store spare batteries in a kitchen drawer. (Are these batteries even any good?)

What about pennies? Some people save their pennies and keep them in a jar on the kitchen counter.

Laundry soap? Excuse me if I'm being presumptuous about the way you should live, but I think that laundry soap belongs close to the washing machine.

Art supplies? Maybe your kids like to draw on the kitchen table (actually, with a little luck, on a piece of paper on the kitchen table), but that doesn't mean you need to keep their supplies in your kitchen. The "Art Department" can be anywhere you choose, and your children can learn to collect and return their art tools to the designated art center, regardless of where they do their artwork. (Better still, buy a fold-up easel, let them create works of art near the designated art-supply storage area, and then teach them to clean up and put away everything, including the easel, when done.)

For each thing you find in your kitchen, ask yourself, "Am I actually in the kitchen when I use it?" If the answer is no, move it to the place where the answer would be yes.

Pots and pans. I bet you have way more than you ever use. And that the cabinet where you store them is so full that it's a chore to fit the just-cleaned pots and pans back inside. I can hear you grunting "uh-huh."

The simple solution is to get rid of the ones you seldom or never use. Many people keep every cooking utensil they've ever owned on the mistaken assumption that one day they'll have to call all their pots and pans into service to feed the entire neighborhood. Has that ever happened? Will it ever happen? No. If for some strange reason you suddenly need to feed twenty-five people, do you think you're actually going to cook for them or order pizza? Think about it. And even if you decided to cook, you couldn't even use all those pots and pans because you only have four burners on your stove.

Right away, without a second's hesitation, you can throw out your dented, rusted, and broken pots, pans, and other cooking utensils. Next you give away the stuff that you haven't used in years, and maybe never used, such as fondue pots, fish poachers, and melon roasters. Finally, you get rid of things you have in quadruplicate, when one or two will do. Colanders, for example. A big and a small should be enough for anyone. Measuring spoon sets. How many things can you measure at once? When you're done with this process, I think you'll find you've made room for the apparatus that actually works and that you plan to use in this lifetime.

The refrigerator. I've saved the worst for last. Refrigerators can be scary things. And I'm not talking just about the science project that you have in there.

Do you really need to keep that frozen breast milk now that your children are entering high school? Will any injury warrant eight ice packs? Why do you need to have three open bottles of ketchup? When was the last time you read that your film needs to be stored in the fridge? How large is your salad dressing collection?

Stop! When was the last time you explored the back wall of your refrigerator and freezer? Haven't been there in a while? That's what I suspected.

In the good old days, the 1960s and earlier, my parents' generation, refrigerators had to be defrosted every once in a while. I remember clearly my mother emptying out the entire refrigerator into an enormous red cooler with sides as thick as a brick (the science of insulation has progressed quite a bit since those days). I'd guess she did this about once a month. Then she turned off the fridge and let the ice thaw, a process that took several hours and required multiple pots and pans.

Meanwhile, she got to throw out all those things that weren't needed anymore and were just cluttering up the shelves. It was a no-brainer to declutter a refrigerator in the 1950s and 1960s, since the more you could throw away, the easier it was to put everything back. This was a very hands-on process: You picked up each item and got the physical sense of it, sometimes in a split second. It either had that "uck" factor and it went, or it was okay, and it stayed. The usual technique was to hold the object with one hand so that the fingers of your other hand could be used to pinch your nose.

Defrosting a refrigerator was the equivalent of moving every month. Remember the last time you moved? How many things you threw away?

Because few people defrost their refrigerators anymore, we're missing a golden opportunity. There happens to be a wire you can cut that will turn off the defrost mechanism, but I suspect nobody reading this book is interested in that. (The defroster component of a frost-free fridge is actually a heater; the nascent ice gets heated and melted away. Now you know that there's a heater in your refrigerator.)

Back to the subject at hand: How do you outwit clutter in your modern, frost-free refrigerator? This can be an especially hard task if there's more than one person in your house who adds stuff to the fridge. Nobody wants to be the person who throws out Daddy's hummus. (Oh, is *that* what's in that container?)

There is actually only one way to outwit clutter in a refrigerator: by stealth. Don't tell anyone what you're up to. Just do it. When they're not at home. Trust yourself and your common sense to distinguish what's still edible from what will never be edible (and maybe from what was never edible to begin with).

Outwitting clutter in a refrigerator is actually one of the easier tasks, and in many ways the most fulfilling. Just drag your garbage can and recycling bin (for the jars) over and go to work.

And remember the Prime Directive of Refrigerator Decluttering: *When in doubt, throw it out!*

Now, what about inadvertently throwing out something that belongs to somebody else? Chances are they won't miss it, but if they do, use this all-purpose (and probably true) defense: "It was spoiled." Who's going to prove otherwise? You've disposed of the evidence, haven't you? And not just in the kitchen garbage can, where it would be easy to retrieve an item. (That would be a stupid mistake, the sort any low-level criminal would make.) You'll do what any thinking, scheming plotter would do and carry out your cleaning raid on the day the garbage goes out to the curb. Perfect timing is when you take out the trash just as the sanitation truck is pulling up to collect whatever you've put out. Now no one can prove anything against you.

You don't need any special advice about what to throw away. That's self-evident. Blue, for instance, is not a typical food color.

Grayish green patterns on food are not normal, either (except on certain varieties of blue cheese, which will carry an expiration date, so go by that). The important thing about outwitting clutter in your refrigerator is to be thorough: Examine every corner, every food item. Start with the upper reaches, in the back corners, and work your way forward on each shelf, and then work down. Everything comes out and gets handled. If it's too yucky to handle, then straight into the trash it goes.

Extra tip: Before you start, just be sure to turn off that tiny little voice in the back of your head that whispers, "Hey, I might still eat that!"

The Bathroom

After kitchens, bathrooms are the second most cited source of unwelcome surplus. A toothbrush, toothpaste, toilet paper, soap, and some towels are all that you really need in a bathroom. (To a certain unnamed cousin: Remember that part about the towels! Tiny embroidered strips of linen do not count as hand towels!) Beyond that, everything else in a bathroom can be construed as clutter. A magazine or catalog by the seat might be okay; a stack of *National Geographics* from 1974 is definitely clutter. If you're over the age of forty, you might have a prescription drug or two, but do you need to keep half a dozen bottles out on the bathroom counter? And at some point, the toothpaste tube really is empty and it's time to throw it out.

To start the decluttering process I advise that you take a look at those things you'd rather not have friends and relatives who might use your bathroom see, such as copies of *Hemorrhoid Today* magazine and boxes of double-dark-chocolate Ex-Lax. Move on to things you'd rather not have to look at on a regular basis.

Either get rid of them or reorganize your covered spaces to make room for them. Use shelf inserts and expanders if you need to. Then deal with those things you actually need to keep at hand but still don't want lined up at the side of your sink or, worse, on the top of your toilet tank. For these essentials a small, attractive wall-mounted rack should do the trick. If it doesn't, then you just haven't been ruthless enough at your decluttering, and you need to repeat the steps above with more vigor this time around.

Shampoo Bottle Blues

Dear Clutter Adviser:

I have a wife and two daughters. Except for our guinea pig, I'm the only male in the house. (And I'm not really sure about the guinea pig.) There are a lot of things that my daughters, ages ten and fourteen, and wife (age I can't tell you) have that I don't ever use. Of all their girl things, what gets in the way the most are their shampoos and conditioners. There must be half a dozen of them in the shower, and another half a dozen on the edge of the tub. These bottles are taking up a lot of room and causing a lot of clutter. Help!

Signed,

Dad

Dear Dad,

What about your shampoo bottle? Is that part of the clutter problem, too, or are you "borrowing" your wife and daughters' shampoo bottles? The reason I ask is that if you're a borrower, you're freeloading on their clutter and are indirectly contributing to your own clutter.

I asked my own wife how she would solve this problem, because I didn't want to give a male bias to the advice. Her reply was, "Suck it up. Women need their shampoos." I can't say that I wholeheartedly agree, but your question touches on a broader issue: How do you declutter something when you have no expertise in that area and, worse, there are other people in your household who are true experts? One way is to monitor the situation. Pay attention to which shampoos are underused, or never used. Point these out to your wife and kids and ask if at the very least they could be put away in a cabinet until needed. Not every shampoo bottle needs to be out all the time. The summertime shampoos can be put away in winter, and vice versa. (I don't really know if there is such a thing as a "summertime shampoo," but I'm guessing that there is because I've seen shampoo bottles that say, "Contains sunscreen to protect your hair from the harmful rays of the sun.")

Now, as a follicularly challenged man, I'm certainly no hair product expert, but I can recommend one solution based entirely on my expertise in decluttering methods: Get a shampoo bottle rack. Bed-and-bath stores sell these coated wire shelves that hang from the shower head. If your female family members are using more bottles than will fit on one of those large-sized racks, what then? Hmm . . . remodel the shower to put in dual showerheads that support two racks? Build a bigger bathroom with more shelf space? Build an all-new bathroom, just for them, and let them put their shampoo bottles wherever they want? You can always throw money at a problem, and in this case, it's easy to throw a lot more money at it than it's worth.

Pill Privacy

Dear Clutter Adviser:

I have a lot of pills (various prescriptions for various things). I don't have enough room in my medicine cabinet, so I keep most of these pill bottles on my bathroom countertop. That presents a couple of problems. First, guests can see what I'm taking, and that's embarrassing. Second, the pill bottles are cluttering up my countertop. What can I do?

Sincerely,

A Prozac Person

Dear Prozac:

Thank you for sharing.

I have good news for you. Why do you have to keep your prescription medicines in the bathroom? Just because you've got a space called a "medicine cabinet" doesn't mean that the bathroom is the only place to store your drugs. In fact, the bathroom may be the *worst* place to keep your meds. That's because bathrooms get hot and humid when people take baths and showers, and the heat and moisture can actually degrade your medicines. (Here's a practical test: Open your aspirin bottle and take a whiff. If it smells at all vinegary, that means that the aspirin has started to break down, and other drugs may be decomposing, too.)

Why not store your drugs in the kitchen? Many medicines need to be taken in the morning, so a kitchen cabinet is an obvious location to store them. Just don't keep your medicine above the stove.

Don't limit yourself to the kitchen, either. Your bedroom is a perfectly good place to keep your pill bottles, and has the added advantage of being accessible only to people who know you really well.

Do You Live with a, er, Slob?

It's probably true that no two people living together are exactly alike in their tolerance for clutter. The classic example is Felix and Oscar—the Odd Couple. But if Felix and Oscar can live together, even with the help of Neil Simon, so, too, can you learn to live with somebody who's not your clutter soul mate.

This issue—how to live with somebody you love who doesn't share your adoration for a clutter-free environment—is in my opinion the most vexing of all the clutter problems I will address in this book.

Opposites attract? If it were only that simple. Opposites may attract, but opposites also try to destroy each other, like matter and antimatter.

In medieval times, alchemists tried to turn lead into gold. They failed to understand that lead, like gold, is an element. Every atom of its being is pure lead. Just the way pure gold is gold in every atom of its being. If you could turn one into the other, then you must have found some way around the immutable laws of physics.

I wish that I had a solution to every single problem (especially that lead-into-gold trick), but I think the problem with most slobs is that they are slobs down to their core. If you could change a slob into a neat freak, the change would be so fundamental that the person would no longer be who he or she really is. Most people know the person they marry pretty well before they commit to a

life together. All I can say, if you're a neat freak who's cho-
sen a slob for a life partner, is that you must have known
about all those slobby habits before you got married. Face
it, those horrible habits are part and parcel of the person
you love. You must accept your love for who he or she is. If
it really *is* true love, then (don't gag yourself with a spoon
here) Love Will Find a Way. That is, if it's possible to make
any kind of path at all through all that awful clutter!

Not to be too discouraging, but I do have a sad story
that's somewhat on point. It's about a mismatched couple
who discovered that they weren't as much in love as they
originally assumed. Albert (I'm calling him that because
of his wild, uncombed shock of hair, like Einstein) was a
professor of Russian at a major American university. He
traveled frequently to what was then the Soviet Union to
do research, to translate, and to lead student groups. One
day in Leningrad, while doing some translation work, he
met a beautiful woman I'll call Melitta (I'm not exactly
sure if that's a real Russian name or just the name of a
coffee filter, but I'm using it anyway), and they promptly
fell in love.

Back in those days (the late 1970s) it wasn't so easy
for a Soviet citizen and an American to get to know each
other well. The Soviet government hardly ever let its people travel to America, and threw any number of road-
blocks in the way of an American who wanted to visit the
Soviet Union too often or stay too long on any trip.
Within just a few weeks of their first meeting, both quickly
realized that they would soon have to decide: either break
it off and go their separate ways, or get married, which
would give them a legal right to ask to remain together
(but still no guarantee that the request would be

granted). Madly in love at that point and determined not to let a totalitarian regime tell them what to do, they went ahead and exchanged vows.

Immediately after that, Albert's visa expired and he had to leave the country.

It took Melitta another six months of battling the Soviet bureaucracy before she won permission to join her husband in the United States. But the glorious day came when at last they could be together again, this time forever. He met her at the airport with a huge bouquet of roses and took her back to his apartment. She walked in the door, expecting to love her new American home with its multiple, modern bathrooms, and its big kitchen full of wonderful appliances, and everything else she knew Americans had in their dream homes.

But to her shock and dismay, she found . . . clutter, horrible, horrible clutter. Albert was a world-class slob. His apartment, while spacious and well equipped with gadgets, also had junk piled upon junk, papers, boxes, stuff stacked up in every spare corner, with layers of dust upon each pile. Melitta didn't know what to say. Over the next few weeks she made feeble attempts at straightening up. But the effort, combined with the stress of having to communicate most of the day in an unfamiliar language and having to adjust to so many strange customs at once, really got her down.

Of course, Albert, a confirmed slob, couldn't change his ways, not even to save his new marriage. What bothered him was, he had married Melitta assuming that she, too, was a slob at heart. He'd seen her apartment in Leningrad and thought he had the proof: It had piles and piles of clutter everywhere, just like his own place back in

America. What he didn't realize was this: Melitta had grown up in that tiny one-bedroom apartment with her parents, both sets of grandparents, and her sister. Although her grandparents and then her parents had died, and her sister had married and moved away, Melitta still had all their possessions. Her apartment was terribly cluttered because it was so small and there was simply not enough space to put away everything in it. If she'd had the space, being a basically very neat person, Melitta would have had no clutter at all.

Within a few weeks it was clear to each that the marriage was based upon a fundamental misunderstanding of the other person's nature. Neat-freak Russian and slobby American had no future together. As soon as was practical, without jeopardizing Melitta's status as an immigrant, they were divorced. And both soon remarried, to people more suited to their personal comfort level of slobbiness/neatness . . . and lived happily ever after.

Yard Clutter

Imagine a painting by Manet. A lush green field edged with flowers. A charming child playing with a hoop. Graceful weeping willows swaying on either side of a shimmering reflecting pool in which float a few water lilies. It's the yard of your fantasies.

Now for the reality, which may include: broken lawn chairs; a rusty shovel; sleds left out in August when the last snow melted in March; a deflated basketball; some badly stacked firewood; a never-used charcoal grill; the new gas grill—the one you plan to use—partially assembled; a hose that leaks a lot; another hose

that leaks just a little; a half-empty bag of mulch; and a stagger-
ing assortment of yard chemicals.

Is it possible to change the reality into the landscape dream?
If you find a talented landscape architect and spend several
thousand dollars, you might just be able to pull it off. But
there's a lot you can do on your own, on the cheap. You may not
end up with that fantasy yard you've been wishing for, but you'll
certainly be a lot better off than you were at the outset. Keep in
mind that not all the ideas below are for everyone. Pick and
choose what works best for your yard conditions, as well as your
preferences.

Pave it. I'm not talking about being like those people who
"paved paradise and put up a parking lot," but rather replacing
some of your yard with an attractive though artificial surface: a
flagstone patio, a wooden deck, a Japanese meditation rock garden, or some other creative idea. Why would you want to do
that and why would it help declutter your yard? The reason you
might want to flagstone (noun as verb, I know, but thwarting
clutter often requires that you break some of the grammar
rules, too) over your grass (or at least a good portion of it) is
that once you have a smooth, solid surface you won't have to
weed it, you won't have to reseed it, or mow it, or fertilize it, and
so you won't have all the paraphernalia associated with those activities needing to be brought out and then put away afterward.
In the extreme, if you were to flagstone your entire yard, you
could do away with your lawn mower, bags of mulch, bottles of
weed killer, watering hoses, fertilizer, lawn food, grass clippers,
and more.

Go organic. Or at least less toxic. Think about what it would
be like to do without all those chemicals, fertilizers, weed killers,
bug sprays, and other ingredients you pour over your yard on a
regular basis. Remember, trees, flowers, and perennial plants all

thrived quite well, thank you, before gardeners started to muck around with Mother Nature. It's not my intention to deliver a lecture about the virtues of a natural, free-form garden versus a clipped and chemically maintained lawn; I just want to give you some thoughts to mull over. When you use fewer chemicals in your yard, you have less to do, and less to worry about. Not bothering with spraying for bugs in March or hunting down every single last slug means that you have more time to enjoy yourself and your yard. When you don't treat your lawn with every chemical known to man, you don't have to have as many bottles, bags, tubs, jars, and other containers around—containers that need to be stored in a child-safe manner and, when used up, disposed of in an environmentally responsible way. By making the simple resolution not to use weed killer, for instance, you've gone a long way toward ridding your yard (and probably garage, too) of a potentially dangerous form of clutter.

Employ your kids. Children are among the biggest yard users. Let them also take on the responsibility of cleaning up after themselves. While children are next to useless when it comes to dealing with certain kinds of clutter, such as office clutter, car clutter, and heavy used-appliance clutter, they certainly have a role to play in helping you reduce yard clutter, especially the kind that they cause. They can be taught to put away jump ropes, sidewalk chalk, soccer balls, and other outdoor play stuff. As they grow bigger and are better able to help with chores like lawn mowing and weeding, they should also be required to put away tools properly when they're done. But you do have to set a good example!

Use the four-seasons rule. The four-seasons rule states that if you haven't used something in your yard at least once during any of the four seasons of the year, it's time to get rid of it. That goes for bent snow shovels and droopy volleyball nets; rakes with missing tines; tulip bulb planters too dull to break the soil; and seed spreaders that haven't sown any seeds in years.

Don't emulate Noah. Unless you've got proof from some indisputable authority that you're supposed to collect all the wildlife in your area, you should do what you can to keep animals at bay. You don't want a yard that attracts squirrels, rabbits, raccoons, foxes, crows, gophers, deer, beavers, alligators, or any other nondomesticated creature that happens to live in your neck of the woods. Wild animals root up bulbs, gnaw through wires and fences, tear up cushions, put holes in the ground and in buildings, and leave their "calling cards" behind, among other forms of damage. To protect your property you'll need to figure out what types of animals you're trying to keep away and tailor your outwitting ideas to the habits of those species. (For detailed help on this problem, look for other titles in the Outwitting series, such as *Outwitting Deer, Outwitting Mice,* or *Outwitting Bears,* or go for them all at once with the help of *Outwitting Critters.*)

The Idle Bicycle

Dear Clutter Adviser:

I don't ride my bike as much as I used to, but I do ride it. I used to do a lot of riding and bought an expensive bicycle to make that activity more fun. Here's my problem: Because it's an expensive bike—more than a thousand dollars—I don't want to keep it outdoors, where it will age quickly. But I feel guilty taking up space in our basement, because I don't ride it that often. What should I do?

Signed,

Still in Shape

Dear S. in S.:

Your case makes the point that there's a close relationship between clutter and our psyches. Often clutter's cause has less to do with the physical objects, and more to do with our mental state. What's holding you back from decluttering your basement by parking your bike outside—like everyone else in your family, I presume—is not what you're planning to do with it, but what you've done. The bicycle has become part bike, part memento. That's perfectly fine, because what we've done is part of who we are. But you shouldn't let what your bicycle represents stop you from the pursuit of happiness. It sounds as though you would be happier if your basement weren't so cluttered, perhaps because it would alleviate your guilt or because your basement would be more usable, or both.

So why not take a compromise step in that direction? You don't have to leave your bicycle outside naked to the elements. Cover it. Buy a tarp or, if it makes you feel better, a customized bicycle cover, and keep that over your bike. The cover will prevent your bike from gathering dust or getting wet; all that will happen to it by being outdoors all the time is that it's going to become warm or cold along with the change of seasons. But trust me on this: Your bike won't mind that at all.

Oh, and there's one potential advantage to keeping your bike outside. Because it's already outdoors, you may be more inclined to ride it.

OUTWITTING CLUTTER TIP

Sometimes it's easier to outwit clutter when there's nobody in the house except for you. Crank up the rock and roll (or something else) and start pruning and organizing.

A Sampling of Yard Clutter Ideas to Start You Thinking (Now Go Make Up Some of Your Own)

- To get rid of visible clutter from hoses and sprinklers, as well as save yourself from the chore of having to move hoses and sprinklers to different parts of your lawn, install an underground watering system. This may be less expensive than you think!

- To keep patio furniture free of bird-doo, hose it off regularly with a high-pressure sprayer. You can also use a hose attachment that allows you to add soap to the spray, so that you can wash and then rinse quickly without the use of buckets and sponges.

- If you can't bring large items (bicycles, barbecue grills, outdoor chairs and tables) inside during bad weather, then buy or make weather covers that protect them from the elements. Large plastic garbage bags, secured with multiple twist-ties, could serve as makeshift tarps.

- Fill your bird feeder with prehulled seeds to avoid having to clean up the mess of hulls underneath. Periodically clean out the feeder to keep molds and fungi from sprouting on the inside.

- Look for creative solutions to your outdoor storage needs. You can buy a giant terra-cotta pot that will hide a coiled-up hose; an outdoor bench with underseat storage to hold sports gear or other outdoor accessories; small tool sheds for your "stuff;" tool racks designed to keep rakes, hoes, and other implements both accessible and protected; impregnable outdoor bins or dispensers to store birdseed, pet food, snow-melting salt, or other pellet-shaped products; and much more. And don't forget hose roll-up systems.

Many of the products mentioned in the bullets above are available in garden shops and hardware stores, but if you can't find something locally, try one of the following catalogs:

Alsto's, 800–447–0048, www.alsto.com
Gardener's Supply Company, 800–427–3363, www. gardeners.com
Gardener's Eden, 800–822–9600 (no Web site)

How to Deal with Important Stuff You Think You Might Need Someday

Now we come to the question of what to do with something you bought many years ago that seemed absolutely essential at the time, but that you haven't used in a long time—perhaps once in the past five years. Let's say you're cleaning out a closet and you come across something that you feel certain you will want to use again one day.

Yeah, like *what?*

Your solar eclipse viewing goggles? Your high school geometry book—just in case you need to consult it to calculate your backyard's acreage? Your army jacket that you can't fit into anymore, even if you do decide to attend your unit's twenty-year reunion (which you have no desire to do, in any case, as long as that killer drill sergeant is still alive and planning to come, too)?

As the tough guy's line goes, *fuggedaboudit.* I'm here to tell you that these things that you expect you'll need once in a . . . solar eclipse . . . you'll never need at all. Get rid of them! Some of the things you think you might need, like your polar explorer's coat, are now moth-eaten, you'll discover. Other things, like your geometry text, will be so outdated as to be useless by the time you get around to using them again. (Didn't anyone tell you that geometry's been replaced by mutiplex invariate deviations?) Or that when you go to use that once-every-ten-years tool, time will have made its power known and the blasted thing will be too corroded with rust to work. Those solar eclipse goggles will be scratched or cracked, too.

Here's the life lesson in a nutshell: Anything you anticipate using once in a decade or half a decade is just dead weight. It either won't work, won't fit, or you won't find it when you want to use it. Or worse: The event will happen and you'll completely forget that you even had the particular apparatus. (Been there, haven't you?) "Damn," you'll say to yourself. "Why did I bother to rent a surfboard? I had one in the attic all this time!" Of course, if you had thought to get it out and had strapped it to your car and hauled it all the way to the beach, the first time you tried to stand up on it you'd have remembered that the fin was damaged. In fact, that's what made you put it away up there in the first place.

Ten Rules of Cluttered Housekeeping by Marjorie Kirslis

1. Vacuuming too often weakens the carpet fibers. Say this with a serious face, and shudder delicately whenever anyone mentions Carpet Fresh.
2. Dust bunnies cannot evolve into dust rhinos if left undisturbed. Rename the area under the couch "The Galapagos Islands" and claim an ecological exemption.
3. Layers of dirty film on windows and screens provide a helpful filter against harmful and aging rays from the sun. Call it an SPF factor of 5 and leave it alone.

4. Cobwebs artfully draped over lamp shades reduce the glare from the bulb, thereby creating a romantic atmosphere. If your husband points out that the light fixtures need dusting, simply look affronted and exclaim, "What? And spoil the mood?"

5. In a pinch, you can always claim that the haphazard tower of unread magazines and newspapers next to your chair provides what in the venerable ancient Chinese practice of Feng Shui is recognized as the "aspect of a tiger," thereby reducing your vulnerability. But try not to roll your eyes when you say this.

6. Explain the mound of pet hair brushed up against the doorways by claiming you are collecting it there to use for stuffing hand-sewn play animals for underprivileged children.

7. If unexpected company is coming, pile everything unsightly into one room and close the door. As you show your guests through your tidy home, rattle the doorknob vigorously, fake a growl, and say, "I'd love you to see our den, but Fluffy hates to be disturbed and the shots are *so* expensive."

8. If dust is *really* out of control, simply place a showy urn on the coffee table and insist, "*This* is where Grandma wanted us to scatter her ashes . . ."

9. Don't bother repainting. Simply collect a few cans of old wall paint and flick wet paintbrushes over the dirty spots, and then tell your guests, "You know the previous owners had Jackson Pollock here before he was famous. He did this painting right on the walls. Too bad he forgot to sign his name . . ."

10. Mix one-quarter cup of pine-scented household cleaner with four cups of water in a spray bottle. Mist the air lightly. Leave dampened rags in conspicuous locations. Develop an exhausted look, throw yourself onto the couch, and sigh, "I clean and I clean and I still don't get anywhere . . ."

OUTWITTING CLUTTER TIP

After twenty years you can throw out all your old college textbooks without any fear. Practically everything in them will be out of date by then. But here's a thought that doesn't take an advanced degree to put into practice for those readers about to graduate: Save yourself twenty years' worth of storage of dead weight by reselling them to the campus bookstore (used-book division) the day after graduation.

Tools

Tools. Can't live without them. And you can't live with them, at least not if your significant other likes to keep his tools by the bed so that they're handy.

From pliers to electric screwdrivers, tools need a place and tools take up room. Tools ought to be reasonably accessible, and some tools need to be handier than others. So where do you put tools? How do you outwit the clutter caused by the spawning of more and more tools? Finding a central place to put all your tools is especially difficult because of all the different sizes, shapes, and weights that tools come in. (Metric or English? Phillips or regular? Has anyone ever used *all* of the socket wrenches in a large set?) For the average tool-owning person, a kitchen drawer won't suffice.

Here's a strategy: First, place any specialized tools close to the thing that those tools are specialized for. Car-related tools come to mind in this regard: All those odd lug nut wrenches can go in the garage. Your jeweler's tools, which you use to repair eyeglasses, can go in your night table drawer, next to the empty glasses case. The Allen wrench should go near the thing that requires an Allen wrench, which may be your bicycle. Do this for all the appliances and devices that require specialized tools, and you may be halfway through your tool collection already.

Next: Keep a pair of pliers, a set of screwdrivers, and a box cutter in various places in your house. (Better still: Make that a single changing screwdriver, which can convert between flat head and Phillips; Phillips also being an invention to help torture people.) I realize that this may sound proclutter, but it will make your life a lot easier if the most commonly used tools are within easy reach, and will actually help you outwit clutter in general. If you have a screwdriver handy, you're more likely to fix something than have that something just sit on a countertop waiting until you to actually walk down a flight of stairs to the basement to rummage among the tools in a large, messy tool chest then emerge with the correct screwdriver, which you must then bring upstairs. Often tools are acquired from one part of a house, then never returned, and you get left-around-tool clutter.

Perhaps the ultimate clutter-thwarting technique for tools is to have a tool pegboard. Many households have an unused wall. Often that's a basement staircase wall, or a wall in the basement itself. Put up a pegboard and hang your tools there. Voilà: instant organization. Not only are your tools out of the way and easily accessible, but you can see what's hanging where, so you don't waste time rooting around in a dark, cobwebby garage for a particular tool.

OUTWITTING CLUTTER TIP

Getting rid of one giant object that you don't use or like—an untunable piano or an irretrievably stained couch, for example—can quickly make a room look a lot less cluttered.

Organize Neighborhood Giveaway Projects

After you've done your kitchen and bathroom and bedrooms, you've got a lot of stuff to get rid of. Once you've put all this effort into culling what you no longer want, you may not want to invest more time in finding buyers for whatever still has value. It's easier in that case to give it away. But you still might have to load things in your car and take them somewhere. That's a lot of effort (especially if some of the things weigh as much as a couch). Much better for you if you can call someone for a pickup. That's usually easier to arrange if you have a multitude of valuable items to offer. Your own house cleanout may not be enough to qualify for door-to-door service, according to the rules set forth by some charitable organizations. But don't be stymied by that. If you have clutter at home, you can bet that other people on your block or in your apartment building have clutter, too. (And their clutter woes may be worse than yours.) If you find that other people in your neighborhood have stuff that they'd like to get rid of—and, more importantly, *give away*— then you may be able to motivate a charity to pick up clothing, books, working toys, and other things you no longer need, on a regular basis. A number of charities have scheduled pickup services, and if an organization in your community doesn't, suggest to them that they should. While it's not necessarily efficient for a charity to drive halfway across town to pick up an old coat or two at somebody's house, it could very well be worthwhile if there's a whole truckload of stuff to pick up.

You may need to coordinate your neighbors to get them to have their donatable clutter ready for the pickup. One system, employed by a charity in Washington, D.C., involves putting the donations in brown paper bags and clearly marking the bags with the name of the charity or tying big yellow tags with the name of the charity onto any item that's too large to bag. This way people can leave their donations on their front porches, or in front of their apartments, and there won't be any worry about the charity's employees picking up their kid's brand-new scooter, instead of the old bicycle that the child has outgrown.

Coordinating this effort isn't as difficult as you might expect. Among the things that you'll need to do or find out are:

- Do any charities already have regularly scheduled pickups in your city? If so, ask if they can add your block to their route.
- What charity will do the pickups?
- When will the pickups be done and in what geographic area?
- How should the donations be bagged and marked?
- What kind of records or receipts are there for tax purposes?

Once you have answers to the questions your neighbors will want to know, get out the word about this new neighborhood activity. You can do this by ringing people's doorbells, dropping off flyers, or posting to your neighborhood e-mail list.

By organizing a regular charity pickup you will have not only gotten rid of clutter (and created a system for outwitting some kinds of clutter on a regular basis), but also turned your clutter into something that helps people in need. As a fringe benefit, you will be promoting community spirit and strengthening your neighborhood—and neighborhood activities that help promote the common good always make your community a better place in which to live.

An A-to-Z Organizer

Maria Gracia wrote this A-to-Z organizer, which I am delighted to print here. She nicely sums up an effective, easy-to-use organizing system.

Organizing A to Z

by Maria Gracia
Get Organized Now!
www.getorganizednow.com

Organizing really can be as easy as A-B-C. Here are twenty-six organizing ideas—one for each letter of the alphabet:

A: Act—Don't put it off until later. If you want to do it, act on it now.

B: Break It Down—Anything you have to do is easier if you break it down into manageable parts.

C: Containerize—Separate and organize your things by storing them in see-through plastic containers.

D: Delegate—You don't have to do everything yourself. Delegate work to associates or family members. Use an outside company to outsource some of your work. Or use technology to your advantage, by delegating to your answering machine, your computer, and so on.

E: Eliminate—Get rid of clutter, both physical and mental. You'll breathe easier and feel a sense of freedom.

F: File—Don't let that paperwork grow into a mountain. File it away in an appropriate place if you need to refer to it again.

G: Give—Give the things you no longer use or love to a favorite charity organization, a family member, or a friend. There are many people who will be thrilled to receive your gifts.

H: Home Sweet Home—Find a home for everything you own, and keep it in its place. When you need something in the future, you'll know its "address."

I: Identify—Before putting items in boxes for storage (or when you're moving) be sure to identify the contents by labeling the outside of the box. Identify papers in file folders by clearly marking the tab of the folder.

J: Judgment—Use your best judgment to prioritize your life. Be sure you're spending the majority of your time on the important stuff.

K: Knowledge—Knowledge is power. In order to effectively organize something, be sure you're using the organizing systems that will work best for you.

L: Lists—Make lists for things you have to do now and in the future. Master lists and to-do lists will help you get things done. Packing lists will ensure you never forget something when you travel. Shopping lists will ensure you get everything you need at the mall. Telephone lists will remind you of everyone you have to call this week.

M: Motivation—A huge part of getting organized is motivation. Once you're motivated, there's no limit to what you can accomplish. Get motivated by designating rewards for your accomplishments, involving family members or friends in your goals, and making getting organized a game. And definitely stop by the Get Organized Now! discussion forum (www.getorganizednow.com) for lots of inspiration and motivation.

N: No—It's so easy to get stressed when you have a million things to do on your plate. If you're beginning to feel burdened with too much to do, learn to say no to some of those things.

O: Order—Rather than living in clutter and chaos, vow to live a more orderly life. You'll know where everything is, and you'll complete whatever you start.

P: Plan and Prepare—While spontaneity every once in a while is fun and perfectly fine, having a good plan and effectively preparing will help you reach your goals and deadlines so you can enjoy maximum accomplishment.

Q: Quality, Not Quantity—It is much better to have a few treasures that you love and enjoy than to have lots of things you don't particularly care for. Always think "Quality over quantity," and you'll simplify your life. Of course, this doesn't apply to money.

R: Reminders—Use little reminder devices throughout the day to help you stay on track. Alarm clocks, timers, e-mail reminders, and sticky notes are all excellent memory joggers.

S: Sell It—Why not make some money by selling some of those possessions you no longer want? Try a rummage sale, consignment shop, or online auction company.

T: Toss—If you don't want it and you can't give it away or sell it, toss it. Make room for the things that you really enjoy, or that make your life easier.

U: Unused Space—Don't forget about the space in your home or office that's so often forgotten about, such as wall space for shelves, hooks for hanging, or space under the stairs.

V: Visualize—Picture how wonderful your life is going to be when you're organized. Then strive to put yourself in that picture every day.

W: Write It Down—Don't try to keep everything you have to remember in your head. Simply write it down and refer to it when needed.

X: X Marks the Spot—Place an X next to each item you accomplish on your to-do list. At the end of the day, add up your X's and celebrate for getting so much done!

Y: You—Don't forget to make time for *You*. Remember, an appointment with yourself—time for you with no interruptions—should be one of the most important appointments in your day.

Z: Zone In—Really define what you're trying to accomplish, so you have a clear picture in your mind.

Parenting and Clutter

4

Birthday Presents and Other Signs of a Cluttered but Happy Childhood

Just when you think you've gotten everything straightened up, your kid has a birthday. The birthday boy or girl isn't ready to play with the stuff yet, and the parents, exhausted from organizing an event that seems comparable to a presidential inaugural, aren't ready to put the stuff away.

It's not just that your child's room, so nicely organized before the party, looks like the warehouse for Toys "R" Us. No, scratch that: The room looks like the product testing center for Toys "R" Us's rejects. The trouble is that birthday presents, along with all their trimmings, have a tendency to remain wherever they were upon opening for a long time to come. Because what child has time to do the Sew-a-Quilt craft set, the Stuff-Your-Own-Bean-Pal beanbag animal creation kit, the Assemble-Your-Own-Portable-Home-Nuclear-Device model weapons-maker set (parental supervision advised), along with the eight or nine other arts and science projects he or she no doubt received before the next birthday rolls around?

There's a lesson here somewhere, but I must tell you, it's not "Ban birthday parties." Nor is it "Write NO PRESENTS, PLEASE" on

the bottom of the invitation. Not unless you want your child to grow up to write a best-selling memoir titled *My Cruel, Heartless Parents* that makes you infamous around the globe.

I'm actually expecting that to happen to a couple I know only slightly. I first got an inkling that the family wasn't quite normal in the clutter department when I was invited to their house for a business meeting with the dad. From the moment I walked through the front door, I was struck by how different the house was. It took me a few seconds to figure out what was wrong with it: It was perfectly clutter-free. Not so much as a Lego out of place (and I'm not talking about just the adult rooms—I'm talking about the kids' playroom, which I saw when given a house tour). In fact, as I walked around, I saw not a single outward sign of the three children I'd been told lived there. No amputated dolls, no trucks missing a wheel, not a single crushed Cheerio underfoot (and one of the kids was a toddler), no leaked stuffing from a torn teddy bear, no half-chewed copies of *Pat the Bunny*, no partially assembled tricycles, no random jigsaw puzzle pieces. Most amazing: *No emergency phone numbers on the refrigerator.* If you're not a parent, this may not sound all that strange to you; if you are a parent, you have to wonder: Are their children holograms? How do they do it? The living room had pristine leather couches, obviously very expensive, and just as obviously untouched by their own children's hands (much less sat on by their little bottoms). There were crystal vases on low tables and other fragile objects everywhere. Even I, a fairly mature adult, felt nervous moving around the oh-so-exquisitely decorated room.

So I ventured to ask: "With three kids under age ten, how do you keep this room looking so . . . [I searched for the right word for a while, because I was about to say "petrified" but settled upon a more tactful choice] . . . neat?"

"Oh, we've *never* allowed the kids in this room," the dad told me. "Nor in the library, nor in my home office, nor in our formal dining room."

"But they must be fairly responsible kids," I observed. "Their playroom is certainly well kept."

"That's because we've trained them to clean up," the dad explained with pride. "If they leave anything on the floor, it gets given away to charity that same day. No exceptions."

"Oh," I said noncommittally, while thinking to myself, "Whoa, Captain Bligh, do you have any clue what kind of mutiny your crew has in store for you when they get big enough and angry enough to explode?" As I'm writing this account, the kids of that fanatically clutter-free household are still preteens, but in a future edition of this book I may have information on the form and ferocity of the rebellion they're certain to launch

one day. You might even read about it in the tabloids. (NEAT-
FREAK COUPLE'S CRAZED KIDS REDUCE MILLION-DOLLAR MANSION TO
RUBBLE!)

In healthy contrast, I offer you a portrait of my own house.
There *are* a few toys out of place. The quantity of stuffed animals
in the stuffed animal bin far exceeds its capacity. A few Barbies
are missing some limbs. There are crayons in the adult pencil
jars. There are stray crayons in more places than I care to re-
count. Occasionally they end up in the dryer (very bad!).
There's glitter that no amount of vacuuming will remove from
the cracks in the floorboards. (Actually, glitter is made of some
mysteriously ineradicable substance. I sometimes wonder
whether the Pentagon has explored its potential as a weapon
against our enemies.) No one would ever call my house "pristine." Nor would anyone who walked in the door doubt that
kids lived here. If fact, they'd probably think we had a dozen.
Truth is, we have only two. And they're pretty good kids. In fact,
they're terrific kids. But neat freaks, they are not.

And we have acknowledged the fact that they never will be.
It's not in their nature. So that leaves us with three choices:

1. Clean up after them on a daily basis.
2. Nag them around the clock to clean up their own mess.
3. Learn to live with a certain amount of clutter until
   they're old enough to leave home.

We do a bit of all three. But it's a constant struggle to keep
up strategies number 1 and 2. The default mode is number 3.
That makes it all "temporary clutter," because we can fix an ending date, about ten years from now when they pack up and go
off to college. In the meantime we tend to focus on the health
and safety side of the clutter problem. We do a good job of
keeping toy cars and skates and other wheeled things off the

Does this look familiar?

stairs. We enforce a rule against any object with sharp edges or points being left on the floor. We don't let the kids snack on anything crumbly or drippy anywhere but in the kitchen, so that food mess will be contained where it is easiest to clean up. We make them wash their hands both before and after eating, so that we don't have chocolate handprints on the wall. And we bribe them with cash rewards whenever they do tackle a big cleanup job in their rooms. (Okay, not the best parenting technique in the world, but whatever works, right?)

I'm not saying that all parents should be as laissez-faire about kids' clutter as my wife and I have learned to be. I do think there's a nice middle ground between that neat-freak family I visited and my own overly kid-cluttered home. At least I've talked to a lot of parents while researching this book who think they've found some solutions to thorny clutter problems. Here are some of the types of kid clutter I'll be tackling in this chapter:

- The stroller that makes your front hall seem so small.
- All those size 4T jumpsuits that your newborn received as gifts.
- Broken crayons and used coloring books.
- Kids' art that doesn't seem like much now but which might be worth something in the future when your shining star becomes a famous artist.
- Board books and other literary works intended for toddlers that still take up room on your preteen's bookshelf.
- The build-a-complete-medieval-castle-with-a-working-drawbridge set with 225 separate parts that are now in 225 separate parts of the house.
- All those worthless little movie tie-in toys that your kids got for free with their Happy Meals.
- Toy parts that prove the theory of spontaneous generation.

Newborn Clutter

Let's get down to business, starting at the logical beginning with newborns. Truth be told, newborns don't need a lot of stuff. They don't need a dozen stuffed animals. They don't need clothes that fit a one-year-old. They're not ready for a swing. They don't need those thirty or forty pounds of diapers that your neighbor gave you when her toddler was toilet-trained. They don't need "educational toys." They don't even really need a crib, yet. Newborns aren't going anywhere; they can't even roll over. Flatten a paper grocery bag and put your newborn on it, and that's where she will stay. I'm not recommending that you put your one-week-old there, but you could, and she'd still be there two hours later.

So the first rule is: When you have a newborn, don't acquire more than you need. If you're not traveling anywhere soon, hold off on getting a portable crib until you feel up to mastering the physics of folding and unfolding the thing (a graduate degree in engineering is not a prerequisite, but it helps). Although almost all parents have a crib waiting for their newborn, a smaller bassinet will work perfectly well for the first few months.

New parents don't really need more than a car seat, diapers, wipes, a changing pad, a small plastic tub, some onesies, some spit-up rags, a stack of receiving blankets, and a camera that works.

That's about it. I feel confident preparing such a minimalist list, because I'm sure that no parent will stick to it. In no time you'll be tempted by catalogs and friends to get a second stroller, an electric baby swing (Why? Can't you rock your baby back and forth all night long? What kind of parent are you, anyway?), pretty pink or blue clothes, soft, fuzzy stuffed animals, cute embroidered blankets, various breast-feeding aids, numerous bottle warmers and sterilizers, a year's supply of Children's Tylenol, a variety of medicine spoons, syringes, (because your first and second attempts to get the Tylenol into the baby will probably end up on the floor), the complete Sesame Street video series, a baby bathtub, baby hiking boots, a mobile for the crib, a mobile for the changing table, a mobile that you haven't set up yet, bathtub toys, a video camera, a digital camera, lots of parenting magazines, and more. Sometimes you may feel you should call up a baby catalog company and simply get it over with: Order one of everything.

Resist that urge. It may be hard, but the right thing to do is to pace yourself. Acquire your baby paraphernalia slowly, in stages, giving yourself time to give away or sell some of the things from the previous stage. Not only will this strategy help you cut down on clutter, but it will also give you time to appreciate the needs of your particular baby. Here's an example:

My wife's friend Emily fell in love with a Maclaren stroller she saw in a baby boutique while she was still pregnant. The top-of-the-line stroller cost three hundred dollars but it seemed to do everything: It adjusted to forty-five different positions, it had a rain cover, it had dual disc brakes, it had two baskets, four cup holders, and whitewall tires. Oops, that last thing was on their car, but you get the idea—this was the SUV of strollers. The only thing it didn't do was fold up small. She got it home to her apartment, and it barely fit through the door. She had no end of trouble steering it along the narrow sidewalks in her crowded, urban neighborhood.

But that wasn't the main trouble. The main thing was that her baby, for about three months after his birth, had a bad case of colic. Anytime after he'd been fed (and newborn babies are fed anywhere from six to twenty times a day), he wanted to be held upright. Absolutely the worst position seemed to be lying down in a stroller. Although the stroller was highly adjustable, it wasn't meant to seat a baby who cannot hold up his head on his own. He cried and cried when put into it, no matter how the seat back was adjusted. Before about five months, the only baby-carrying device he seemed happy to be in was a Snugli, a cloth sack that held him upright with his head nestled against his mother's chest. So the stroller sat unused, blocking their small apartment hallway for nearly half a year.

It wasn't until Emily and her husband moved to a large house in the suburbs that they had space for the stroller that they still used only on rare occasions. By the time they moved, their baby could sit up on his own and no longer was bothered by colic; also by that time they had acquired another stroller, the "umbrella" type that can fold up very small and be kept tucked out of the way in a closet when not in use. The model they bought, which they chose because it was the lightest and easiest to fold up, cost only forty dollars. They used it constantly until their son outgrew it and then used it again for their daughter, and then gave it away to another relative, who's getting good use out of it to this very day. The expensive stroller they eventually sold to a consignment shop (it really was in "like new" condition, five years after Emily bought it, but they barely got thirty bucks for it—less than a tenth its original price).

The point is: Know your lifestyle and your baby and yourself, before you buy. A big, protective stroller may look great in the store, but if your baby doesn't like it, what good is it? Because it's doubtful you'll be able to talk the salesperson at a baby products store into letting you take out a stroller for a "test drive" around the block with your baby, you might try to find a friend with a comparable model and ask to borrow it for an afternoon. That's the closest you'll be able to get to matching the product to your baby.

Now for another example: the baby bathtub. This time I'll give you the benefit of my own (in)experience. We were given the baby tub as a gift about a month before our first daughter was born. (we had asked for a tub.) It was a large, elegant thing, made in Italy and all that. It consisted of a tublike container about four feet off the ground. Beneath the tub were two shelves for towels, washclothes, rubber ducks—stuff like that. There was a hose that let you drain the tub into a sink or into another bathtub.

I have to say that the baby bathtub looked like a handy invention. Only thing is, we didn't need it: The tub just cluttered up our bathroom, which was already on the slippery slope to becoming a kid's bathroom.

If we had been able to wait a little while before getting the bathtub, we would have realized that we never needed it, despite its sleek Italian curves. Why not? Well, you can bathe a newborn quite well in the little plastic basin the hospital gives you to take home for free. When they're older —surprise!— they can actually use the same bathtub you do!

I think the same can be said for numerous toys, clothes, second strollers (it's not as if you can use both at the same time, or you even need a "summer stroller" and a "winter stroller"), infant books (sure, one or two books about farm animals might be fun, but keep in mind that you can really do the same thing as these books by reciting the words "duck," "goat," "cow," "chicken," "rooster," along with the appropriate noises for each, blankets (if you think you need more than two or three blankets, then what you really need is a better heating system), and a plethora of so-called educational products.

Do yourself a big favor—and this tip doesn't have to do with just thwarting clutter—avoid acquiring too many toys that beep, buzz, chime, and sing either the Barney or the Teletubbies theme song. I don't think I need to go into much explanation about why.

OUTWITTING CLUTTER TIP

Don't know what to do with the abundance of kids' artwork that comes home from school? Take digital pictures of each piece and "give away" the original paper versions.

Seven Strategies for Coping with Kid Clutter

If the mantra for outwitting clutter with newborns is "Wait," what about when the newborn becomes a crawling baby and all of a sudden you need things like electric outlet protectors, cabinet locks, industrial-strength laundry stain removers, electronic fences, and motion-activated detector cameras? Now the mantra changes to "Think . . . and think again." The more you buy, the more you're going to have to do something with later on. It's harder than you think to throw out some toys or baby devices: After all, you *might* need it for a second child, and besides, how can you throw out something that cost so much? (The quick answer to that question is to auction it off on eBay, or hold a yard sale.)

I know it sounds rather simplistic to say, "Don't buy what you don't need," but it's so much harder to put this saying into practice—especially when it comes to toys—once your children are old enough to understand TV commercials. How many times can you hear "I want thaaaaaat" before you give in out of sheer desperation to get them to stop whining? You know they're being brainwashed by those devils in suits who work for advertising companies, and yet, like the parents of any innocents in one of those horror movies about the demonically possessed, you haven't the heart to confront your own child's greed. So you give in. And the next thing you know you're damned to Clutter Hell for eternity.

Unless the exorcist shows up in time. Hey, I think that's me. Okay, get a grip on the cover of this book, close your eyes, point at the TV screen, and chant: "No power. You have no power here." And turn it off! Your children will be cured. Well, not without some pain. You may have to repeat the exorcism process a few times. You may have to throw away the remote. Eventually, if you stand your ground and hang tough, you will win. (Just be sure not to let their possessed friends re-initiate them into the devilish cult of Never-Ending Toys.)

Now, suppose you were weak once and you gave in too often and have already acquired far too many toys? The question is: Is it possible to get rid of some of them? You may think I'd say yes. I tell you to throw out so many things in this book, you may have begun to imagine I'd say yes to *anything*. But once a toy has won a child's heart, it's like a pet. You don't send Fluffy to the pound just because he grew up to be a bit bigger than you expected when you brought him home, do you? And it's not just that; it's also true, perhaps to a surprising extent, that the other adult in your house has made an emotional investment in keeping the kids' outgrown toys. I've been there myself. It happened when my wife proposed throwing out a set of cardboard box bricks that our kids used to use to build forts in the basement. True, our kids no longer play with these box bricks, and true, they take up an annoying amount of space in our basement—but dammit, I spent something like fifty-four hours assembling those bricks, *without any instructions in English whatsoever.* I did it by a combination of intuition, sweat, and guesswork, using every curse word I ever knew and inventing twenty more in the process. A lot of my soul went into giving my kids those bricks. And they're damn well going to keep them till they're my age, at least.

There is a lesson here for others, I hope. There will come a time when you'll want to throw something out but will be stymied by the opposing spouse. Don't fight about it; let it go. When it comes to parenting, presenting a united front to your children is a lot more important than getting rid of this or that item of clutter.

However, those of you who have not yet acquired a basement full of kid stuff should know that, as with heart disease, prevention is your best cure. What you don't have in your house, your children won't miss.

But let's say you fail to hold the line against clutter early on and now find yourself fighting a lonely rear-guard action against the pileup of toys, toys, and more toys. Take heart; all is not lost. There are still things you can do to keep yourself from drowning in toys. A few "better late than never" strategies for the over-toyed among us:

First strategy: Create storage space before you buy. When contemplating bringing home a toy with many small parts and accessories, establish a bin or drawer where the toys and all its components will go. Without such a plan, soon after purchase the main part of the toy will drift away from its parts, and you will end up with the engine part of the toy semi in one room and the tractor-trailer part and all its cargo in some other room, two floors distant. You may find the doll in the dollhouse, but not the doll's dog (one of the doll's many accessories), nor the doll's dog's leash and collar (hard to believe, but it's true: Doll accessories have their own accessories). Once a toy is separated from its part, your child may ignore it and let it sit unused until somehow the parts magically reunite themselves. In other words, it will turn from plaything to clutter.

Second strategy: Control quantity. Once you have the type of toys that come in different sets (Legos, Lincoln Logs, K'NEX, BRIO Blocks, and other building sets), hold firm against adding set after set. Never buy more than can be contained by the toy bin that you've already established for the toy (as per the strategy above). Don't let each child maintain his or her separate set in a separate part of the house. Keep everything together. And don't walk around barefoot at night anywhere that stray pieces could conceivably lurk. Plastic edges feel like sharpened metal against your tender toes in the dark.

Third strategy: Broken toy management. When it comes time to throw out that truck with a missing wheel or the game with more than 50 percent of its pieces missing, don't succumb to the false promise that the "pieces will turn up soon." For as long as you hang on to the main item, they will remain in toy limbo. Yes, they will turn up eventually, but it's a variation of Murphy's Law that the missing toy part will only be found once you've thrown the rest of the set away.

Fourth strategy: Limit the number of jumbo toys. I'm talking about things such as jungle gyms, trampolines, indoor toboggan chutes, life-sized stuffed giraffes, elephants, and gorillas, battery-powered child-sized cars that go up to fifteen miles per hour (a variant on the adult golf cart), and indoor castles that have a real working drawbridge and are surrounded by a plastic wading pool moat.* A good rule of thumb is, one really big thing per child per half decade (or fewer, if you have three or more children). Bicycles and scooters may be treated as exceptions.

Fifth strategy: Buy only what's age-appropriate. The problem isn't that your children might get a toy that's too advanced, too sophisticated, or too sexy, but that toys that are the wrong age for your children are never played with and just take up space (the very essence of clutter). You may or may not agree philosophically that Barbies are inappropriate for little girls, but I

---

*If you doubt that all of these things exist, check out the F.A.O. Schwartz catalog or visit www.fao.com.

think there's little disagreement with the proposition that a one-year-old isn't going to get a lot from owning a Barbie. All that's going to happen is that sometime between now and age two the Barbie will be dismembered. Believe me, I know. In a short time you'll have various body parts all around the house, and you'll start to wonder if your child's future is in forensic medicine. And what's a two-year-old going to do with a chess set? By the time your daughter is actually ready to play chess (and interested in it), all the chess pieces will have migrated to other "games"—the knights will have become part of a "fairy playground," the rooks will be part of a "magic kingdom," and the pawns will be attached upside down to various surfaces with Silly Putty. What to do when given a present your child is too young to enjoy? Here are three good choices: (1) Put it away in a storage space until your child is the right age for the present— and don't forget to take it out before your child is *too* old! (2) The next time you need to give a present to an older child, don't go shopping—you've already got a gift on hand. (3) Take it back to the toy store and exchange it for something your child can use right now.

Sixth strategy: Get rid of outgrown toys. On the flip side of the "wait until they're old enough" rule is the dictum that you should give things away as soon as your children are too old to bother with the thing in question. I'm not talking about their favorite "blankie" or their first teddy bear: Keep that for posterity (but do put it away in a mothproof case). I'm talking about those toddler board books. Why are they still taking up room on your kid's bookshelf when he's reading *Catcher in the Rye*? You have a local library, I'm sure. Most libraries gleefully accept books—and videos—in good condition. Call to ask if they would like a donation. We've done this on a regular basis and it's made a significant dent in bookshelves. After all, now that our kids are seven and ten, there's no chance anyone will ever watch those Barney videos again. (I'm sure we would have been quite a bit better off if we'd *never* watched them in the first place.)

When we made our first secret donation, we hadn't considered the one potential side effect. It wasn't that our daughters might notice that *Pat the Bunny* was AWOL. Rather, when we took our kids to the library a little while after donating some videos, their eyes naturally went to a video rack in the kid's section, and they said, "We have these same videos!" It was a close call, but our daughters never made the connection. One day, if they ever read this book, they'll find out what a terrible, awful, horrible thing we did, but until that day, it's a secret that's worked well.

Seventh strategy: Neighborhood swap meet. Think of creative, new ways to reduce your kid clutter level. One that I like a lot is the neighborhood book and toy swap. If you try this method (I hope this goes without saying), you *must* leave with less than you came with. It does no good to attend a book or toy swap only to end up with more stuff than you had originally brought in. This is a matter of brute willpower: *You must resist* your child's inevitable demand to come back with too much. As a general rule of thumb, it's a good idea to end up with no more than half of what you came to the swap with. Tell your children that the swap lets other kids enjoy many more toys and books if you don't take home too much. You might also consider losing the shopping bags you brought your toys and books over with. Whip out a zipper-lock bag and say, "We can only take home what fits in here." (That trick may only work one time, as your child may insist in bringing along an empty shopping bag next swap.)

Remember, the successful outwitting of clutter is a product of both major efforts and little steps. You certainly would accomplish more on the road to a clutter-free life by throwing out thirty old toys or books in one fell swoop. But unless you enjoy riots, that's not always an option. Major steps aren't always possible, which is why scheming people like me invent smaller, more clever steps. A swap accomplishes your goal, toy reduction, without unleashing hysteria. Indeed, you might even get your kids to enjoy swapping books and toys, even if they end up with fewer than they started with. To a child, a swap means something *new*, and quality is sometimes more important than quantity. When kids trade toys with their siblings, the exact number of toys is often important—"Sally got more toys than I did!"—but swaps are different.

If your neighborhood recreation center, kids' club, or play group doesn't run them, it's easy to set one up yourself. Call a dozen or so parents of kids about the same ages as your own. Tell them the ground rules: Things to be swapped must be in good condition; everything left over will be given to a designated charity; only things of interest to the age group in question should be brought; and so forth. It's a good idea to pick a central location—a neighborhood playground, or someone's large front porch—and set up cookies and lemonade for all comers (or the kids could sell what they've made). Give the idea a try—it's lots of fun.

Tub Toys

Dear Clutter Adviser:

Years ago we moved our daughters, now ten and eight, to bedrooms on the third floor of our house, where they have their own bathroom and tub. But Julie and Sharon still like to take baths in the Jacuzzi in our bathroom, mostly because it's so big. That's okay with us, the parents, but what we don't like is that their bath toys are still in our bathroom. How can we get rid of those toys without moving our kids to tears?

Signed,

Weak Willed

Dear Willy:

The solution to this problem depends on how important it is to reclaim your bathtub. Children and clutter are a curious mix and hard to separate. For the most part, kids don't see clutter the same way that adults do. To children, clutter is fun because there are more places to hide things, because you can play games with clutter, and because you may discover something new and fun in the clutter. Kids also don't like change. Alter *anything* and your daughters are likely to object.

So here's what I propose. Tell your kids that you're going to move their toys to their own bathroom. Julie and Sharon will most likely raise a tempest in a bathtub, but that will pass. Chances are that they'll want to take a bath with their toys that very night, so while you may have angry kids for a time, at least you'll have angry clean kids.

To soothe their souls, point out that many of the toys are actually either broken or ones that they don't play with anymore.

Julie and Sharon will protest that, too, but the truth of it will eventually sink in. To help them realize that not everything is worth keeping forever, enlist their help in moving the toys upstairs. Once they are recruited to join in the process, they'll likely start to pick out items it's not necessary to relocate. They might even be glad to get rid of that mermaid with the soap-scum-coated hair—the kids no longer like to touch it. The boat that tips to one side when you want it to float can sail right over to the trash can.

Next, start pointing out types of toys that are no longer usable for other reasons. As a plumbing protection matter, you need to throw out any toys that don't dry quickly, tend to get stuck in the drain, get mildewed, or are in any other way unsatisfactory for bathtime play. Keep in mind that you don't need to throw out all those bath toys at once—or even move them from your bathroom to the kids' tub in one transfer. If you do it a few toys at a time, over a period of several weeks or even months, your children will accommodate themselves to the changes much more easily than if you swooped in and triaged and moved their toys all in one fell swoop.

OUTWITTING CLUTTER TIP

Recycle toys in your own house. Take advantage of your toddler's short memory by periodically rounding up a few excess toys and stashing them in the basement or in a toddlerproof cupboard. Then, a few months later, bring out the toys as brand new.

Fast-Food Toy Clutter

I'm putting this type of clutter in its own section because it's so insidious. Many years ago some marketing genius (or, more accurately, evil genius) at the McDonald's corporate headquarters came up with the idea of packaging a few of the most kid-popular menu items (a burger, fries, and a drink) together with a cheap plastic toy. Thus was born the "Happy Meal" and its many imitators. Years later, many families find their houses and cars littered with pieces of miniature Barbies, Hot Wheels cars, itty-bitty Beanie Babies, body parts of Inspector Gadget dolls (because you must go back once a week for eleven weeks to collect all the parts to assemble a complete Mr. Gadget doll), and no end of pint-sized plastic replicas of movie characters from every major production that Disney and Pixar Studios have ever turned out.

Have no doubt: Every single bit and piece that's ever been packed inside a Happy Meal box is pure, unadulterated clutter. The solution: Never take your kid to a fast-food place. "Get real!" you say. Okay, take them, but don't get roped into the food-plus-toy deal. Order the kids' food à la carte. That way you can also split a single order of fries among all the kids, cutting down on the amount of fat they consume at the same time you fight clutter. If they order from the full menu, rather than just what's available for the kids' special meal deal, it may just be possible to steer them toward more healthful choices for the main course, as well.

If that strategy proves too hard to enforce, here's another approach: Get them the Happy Meal, let them play with the toy at the table during the meal, but then encourage them to leave it behind for the next child when they're done. If you can get them used to this idea from an early age, they should be okay with it for the long haul. Not many of the fast-food toys are the sort kids are all that sorry to give away. In fact, even from the kids' point of view, they're pretty recognizable as junk.

Now for my final (wimp-out) answer: If you must take the toys home, establish a single bin labeled FAST-FOOD TOYS AND PARTY FAVORS. Into this bin toss all those annoying little plastic things the kids bring home from parties as well as whatever you bring back from outings at fast-food places. I think you'll quickly discover that once a toy is dumped into this bin, it's rarely taken out and played with again. You can then periodically cull what's in the bin to get rid of old, boring, broken toys, and make room for the new. I promise you that whatever you throw out won't be missed.

OUTWITTING CLUTTER TIP

Think of eating your kids' Halloween candy as part of the effort to outwit clutter. (Now you have a good excuse.)

Things to Put Kids' Things In

You've read my recommendation that you get bins for toys. I'm just using the word *bins* as a shorthand for "anything that works to sort and stow kids' stuff." When you read the word *bins,* don't just think of plastic tubs with tops. Think creatively. Kids' things (not just toys but also clothing, school supplies, and other possessions) can be put into many different types of organizing arrangements, including:

- Furniture with shelves, drawers, cabinets.
- Stacking cubes, plastic milk crates, or other boxes.
- Shoe bags.
- Hampers (look for divided ones that work as sorters).
- Net hammocks (especially good for hanging over the bathtub so that bath toys will dry).
- Racks, pegboards, or other types of wall organizers.

You can buy these products at bed-and-bath stores, at hardware stores, at discount stores, or at specialty kids' furniture stores, as well as from baby and child catalogs. Try these:

The Right Start, 800-548-8531, www.rightstart.com
One Step Ahead, 800-274-8440, www.onestepahead.com
Sensational Beginnings, 800-444-2147, www.sb-kids.com

OUTWITTING CLUTTER TIP

Here's a method of getting rid of excess baby toys that also works to improve family relations. Ship some of your overabundant fun stuff to Grandma's house. Fill a few cardboard boxes with stuffed animals, rattles, and other playthings that aren't everyday favorites. If you've got too much stuff, your baby won't miss what you clear out. The next time you leave your baby at Grandma's, she has all kinds of amusements you know are safe and fun. Grandma will thank you, too, for sharing the goodies.

Assign Your Kids Outwitting Clutter Tasks

From the moment they can crawl, children create clutter. (You might argue that from the moment they're born, children create clutter. But that's not true: Until they crawl, you, the parents, are the sole clutter creators. Think about it.)

Assigning your children anticlutter jobs will not only help keep your house cleaner but also teach them that outwitting clutter isn't that difficult to do. You may help your kids to develop lifelong anticlutter habits.

As you work on a list of things your children can do around the house, think *small*. They can't handle the big stuff yet. Don't give them assignments that involve moving more than they can comfortably carry. Take their schedules into account—don't interfere with their homework, for example. Give them advance warning about the task they're asked to perform, and don't give them last-minute marching orders, even if they forget the job. Don't assign impossible tasks, such as "organize the front hall closet once a month." If you can't handle something, then you can't expect your kids to be able to.

This sounds like a long list of don'ts, but the prohibitions are as important as what your kids should do. Parenting is difficult enough without your creating another battleground. Make the anticlutter work comfortable, enjoyable, nonstressful, and even interesting and challenging, if you can.

One other point: Turning your children into outwitting clutter allies is different from having them take care of what they're supposed to do on a daily basis, such as picking up after themselves, putting their homework in the right place, helping clear the dinner table, and so on. These are *chores*. What I'm talking about here are anticlutter roles.

Now, on to specifics. Here are some ideas for anticlutter projects your kids can handle:

Put loose change into coin rolls. You can even let your kids take a percentage of the rolling, or all of it, if you're generous. In our house, we have a policy that says if our kids find loose change on the floor and they pick it up, it's theirs.

Sort the laundry. My kids actually would prefer to do this task themselves than let either my wife or me handle it. That's because neither one of us is very good at remembering which daughter owns the pair of panda socks and which owns the penguin socks. They complain, "Daddy! You put *her* socks in my sock drawer *again!*" "Fine," I quickly learned to respond, "then you do the sorting yourself." And they do.

Declutter their bookshelves. Few kids like to part with their old toddler books, especially any that were bedtime favorites, like *Goodnight Moon* or *Where the Wild Things Are*. It's fine to hang on to these, but there's no sense in saving every board book they've ever owned. If you meet resistance, appeal to your child's best charitable instincts. Tell her that some child whose family can't afford books will learn to read on her old books and have a better future because of her generosity. Kids' books can be given to libraries or to many overseas or domestic educational charities. Also, many schools and religious institutions put on an annual used-book drive. If the idea of doing a good deed doesn't move your child to part with her old books, then what about the profit motive? Let your kids set up a street-corner book stall (may be combined with a lemonade stand and cookie sale) to sell their old books and keep the profits.

Weed patrol. Have your children participate in ridding your yard of weeds. They can pull up weeds on a regular basis (only if you don't use pesticides) and deposit the weeds in the trash. It's actually the second part of the process that's the most important: Weeds should be put in the correct trash receptacle, because it's easy just to yank up a weed and leave it on the grass.

Collect recyclables. Through constant indoctrination in their school social studies programs these days, most American schoolkids get turned into radical environmentalists. At least that's the way it's seemed in this neck of the woods. An unsuspecting parent can never casually toss a newspaper or a cardboard box or a can of anything without some hypervigilant child (usually your own) objecting, "You could've recycled that!" We do like to recycle what we can, but our kids are willing to do a lot more—and we let them. I get a lot of products through mail order and other shipping services. My kids are the ones to put the Styrofoam "peanuts" in plastic bags and take them down to our local UPS center, which accepts them for recycling. They also deflate the air from air-packed shipping cushions so that they don't take up as much space in the landfill. They chop up the cardboard shipping boxes into smaller, flat pieces so that they can go out with the newspapers to be picked up at curbside. They wash out plastic bottles and glass jars and put them in the correct recycling bins. And sometimes they rescue from the trash can jars and cans that I put there without checking their recyclability, and put them in the correct bin. I may make fun of their fanaticism, but I really do admire their efforts and their spirit.

Chore Charts

Assigning your kids' chores through charts works in some families. (Not ours, that's for sure!) If you use charts, don't make them too detailed, too complex, and certainly don't make the charts impossible to complete. Keep these chore charts manageable. You don't need to lay out your own charts; there's an excellent Web site with a variety of charts you can print and use: Chartjungle. Just waltz over to www.chartjungle.com/chorecharts.html and print whatever you need.

Everything in Moderation

Actually, I don't believe that's *always* the case. Cigarettes are not something that should be consumed in moderation. Same for arsenic.

But this aphorism does ring true when the subject is clutter and parenting. Let me give you a for instance, a peek into the mind of an extreme anticlutter fanatic. Here's a message I found on an e-mail list for the clutter-challenged:

My kids are getting *no* toys, books, or movies for Christmas this year. They don't need any. Instead, I have a couple of board games (they don't have any), and will buy some birdseed for the bird feeder (they love to watch them eat; we have had around a hundred birds out there all at once eating) and some drawing paper so they stop using up the printer paper. I have a couple of other small things stashed that they'll get also. If I buy them anything else, it will probably be food of some sort. A package of cookies they would enjoy and it wouldn't be around for very long. 'Course, my kids would be happy with apples too. The girls will also be getting a newly organized and streamlined room that even they can keep clean. The boys don't have a problem with theirs. It stays clean as long as the girls don't go in it.

As the riddle books say, "What's wrong with this picture?" In short, everything. This mother has let her fear of clutter control her life and her home and ruin her children's holiday. Just my opinion, of course, but when you make thwarting clutter the overriding mission in your life, you are going to make the lives of everyone else pretty miserable. Children need to be children; they need holidays, and to a certain extent children need to have a little clutter. Pretending that you can have a completely clutter-free home while you have children is like thinking that at age one your child can be completely out of diapers. I'm sure it is possible to get a twelve-month-old to use the toilet (after all, cats can be taught to), but that's not to say that it's a good idea.

Moderation. Consideration. Compassion. All of these must be an integral part of the way you deal with clutter and kids.

Homework Overflow

Dear Clutter Adviser:

My kids like to do their homework in the kitchen. That's okay with us, because at least they do their homework promptly. The problem is that they leave all their stuff on the kitchen table, so that when it's time to pre-pare dinner, I also have to move their books and papers to someplace else (just shifting clutter). I don't want to discourage my daughters from do-ing their homework right away, but I do want them to stop creating new clutter in the kitchen. I know what you're going to say: "Tell them to clean up their homework as soon as they're done." Well, that's just what I do say, but then my kids often reply, "We're not done yet . . ." The prob-lem is that they don't necessarily finish their homework by the time I need to take total control of the kitchen.

Signed,

Who's the Boss?

Dear Boss,

And I use the term *boss* loosely, because you're apparently ab-dicating that role to your children.

Now, I happen to be a parent of school-age children, too, so I understand your plight, but in order to accomplish what you want in the way of outwitting clutter, you need to develop concrete, effective, and workable rules. The rule you've fash-ioned obviously doesn't work. Your rule "Remove your books and papers when you're done" is the *wrong* rule, because your kids haven't finished their homework when you hope they'll be done.

You need a much better, more appropriate rule, such as "All books and papers must be out of the kitchen by 6 P.M. or else no lima beans with your supper." Your kids also need to know where the homework goes by that 6 P.M. deadline. That's up to you, boss. If it's okay with you for them to reclaim the kitchen table as soon as the dinner dishes have been cleared away, then create a holding pen for homework-in-progress and tell them that's where the books, worksheets, and notebooks will be kept while the table is unavailable. A better solution (to my way of thinking) would be that each child must bring her homework stuff to her own desk or other space in her own room and finish the homework there. That way you'll never face the problem of unfinished homework left out on the kitchen table all night long, taking up your breakfast space.

5

Clutter in All the Wrong Places

The Tough Stuff

This chapter is about lots of different types of clutter, the hard-to-organize clutter, the type that reasonable people can reasonably argue must be treated in certain ways. I'm talking about the catchall term *miscellaneous*. It stands for (or should I say covers for?) a multitude of things. Odds and ends, bits and pieces, things that don't logically belong in any one room, or that some might say don't logically belong in a home at all. This type of clutter can make dogmatic organizers stand their own ground: "Organize it this way or else the anticlutter cause is lost." I take a more laid-back approach: "Experiment with these tough clutter problems and use whatever method works for you."

Instruction Manuals

With virtually every new purchase these days comes an instruction manual. (Never mind how incomplete or poorly translated that manual is; that's not the point.) Many products, formerly uncomplicated and run by common sense, now involve fifty pages of diagrams and details. Everything from programming a

VCR to setting your alarm clock calls for lengthy instructional literature. We just purchased a new vacuum cleaner and I couldn't get it to operate without first reading the manual (translated from German). A vacuum cleaner, of all things, requiring a manual! Raise your hands if you own at least one digital clock (including your car's clock) that you can't set forward or backward as Daylight Saving Time changes without consulting the manual. Does your telephone have more features than you'll ever use? Have you encountered a flashlight you can't even turn on? Do you own any products that require you to press two buttons simultaneously in order to make something happen? So here we are, not on the Information Superhighway, speeding along our merry way, but in the clutter of instruction manuals, bogged down on diagram 2(a)-iii. If there's one truth to the world, it's this: Lose the instruction manual and be prepared to suffer with your appliance's clock blinking 12:00.

You're not alone, either, if you can't find the manual. Or more precisely, you can find every manual *except* for the one that you need.

There are really only two good ways to organize instructions:

1. Keep them all in one place labeled clearly with the word INSTRUCTIONS.
2. Keep them with the appliance.

There are a couple of tricks to each of these two techniques.

If you decide to keep all your instructions together, make sure that the bin is big enough to hold them all (and is very expandable). Otherwise, you'll find yourself cramming new manuals in where they don't fit, scrunching up other manuals, and ending up with torn pages. And the particular troubleshooting tip you need will invariably be on the page that's torn beyond legibility.

If you decide to keep the manual with the appliance, you need to keep it safe but still accessible, but somewhat hidden from view (otherwise it looks like clutter). I slip the washing machine manual into a waterproof plastic zipper bag and then tape it to the side of the machine. I fold the VCR manual so that it fits neatly into an empty VCR box, label the outside MANUAL, and keep it on the shelf with the movie tapes. The manual to my printer sits underneath the paper tray, folded open to the page telling me how to cancel a print run. That way I don't have to let the printer finish a three-hundred-page job while I'm frantically searching through the index of the forty-eight-page manual to find out how to "cancel print job."

There is a third way I haven't mentioned yet. It's not a strategy for keeping your manuals. It's a bit extreme, not for everyone, but it certainly fits in with the anticlutter ethos of this book: *Throw all instruction manuals out.*

"What?" you cry. "Then when the VCR tape won't eject, I won't know what to do, and the machine will just sit there, uselessly hooked up to the TV, having become a large, black piece of clutter."

Ah, but you can still find the troubleshooting help you need if you search through cyberspace. Most manuals are available online at places like livemanuals.com. If you don't find what you need, try calling the manufacturer's toll-free number. You may be directed to a Web address to find the manual you need, or you may be sent a replacement manual in the mail. Of course, none of this guarantees that you will be able to understand the instructions when you get them. But that's no different from having saved the paper manual.

Hobby Stuff

I have a hobby. Hobbies tend to cause a lot of clutter. In fact, I am willing to wager that *all* hobbies cause clutter, even ones that you wouldn't suspect are clutter prone. For example, I used to fly airplanes upside down for fun. I didn't collect airplanes—that would have really been a space problem. But aviation requires stuff: headset, portable aviation computer, charts, parachute, more charts, batteries, sunglasses, flashlights, portable aviation transceiver, life jacket, airport guides (it's important to know which small airports have rest rooms, especially when you're flying a plane without one), weather maps, and more. I'm sure sailing is the same, or maybe worse. Okay, these are big equipment hobbies. But look at a smaller-scale pastime such as chess. There will be several chess sets—maybe a big collection of them—as well as chess books, special chess notation paper, timers, and a table. Then there are those cute little chess knick-knacks and accessories people give a hobbyist as gifts: chess salt and pepper shakers, chess calendars, chess notebooks, chess pens, chess ties, chess hats. Videotapes of great games (that may or may not ever be viewed). Chess magazines (twelve issues a year). Chess-piece-shaped pasta, sitting in a box in the kitchen cupboard waiting for someone to remember to make a meal of it sometime when the regular players come over for a game.

I repeat: Every hobby generates clutter. This includes sports hobbies. Take soccer. Front halls get filled with muddy cleats, kneepads, jerseys, and things that resemble socks.

If you look around your house, you'll find that whatever your interest, there's some clutter to go along with it. Do you collect books? Pez dispensers? Do you tape reruns of *Friends*? (Where do all those videotapes go?)

Recently I've started to enjoy digital photography. You'd think that anything digital would be relatively clutter-free, but think again. There's the camera, of course. But there's also the camera bag, lens-cleaning paraphernalia, batteries, memory cards, manuals, discs, memory card reader, cable, more discs, and other stuff. Then even digital photographers like to print their best shots. So I've got the special photography paper and a separate printer I use when I turn a digital photo into a paper photo, plus a cutting board and the stiff cardboards I use to mail the photos I've printed to my nonwired relatives and friends. And none of this takes into account the huge amount of digital clutter that digital photography creates on my computer.

But the hobby I want to talk about here is music. Music is especially clutter prone. It's not just the amount of space that CDs take up, which I'll get to in a moment. It's also the fact that many people have music in more than one format: vinyl LPs, cassettes, CDs, mini discs, DATs, eight-tracks (for a few), memory sticks, mini CDs, and DVDs. With more formats to come, I'm sure. Although most listeners have music in more than one format, each of us probably has one preferred listening format: While you may have cassettes lying around, it's likely that you play your CDs many more times than you play those cassettes. Or your LPs. But you still can't bear to throw out those other formats, even if you last listened to something from another format at the time of our last moon landing. (That was the heyday of eight-tracks, by the way.) And far be it from me to suggest that you part with your favorite tunes. In fact, one of the differences between this book and some of the other anticlutter books out there is that I will never, never insist that you throw out something just because you don't use it anymore. Outwitting clutter isn't rigidly prescriptive. It's more clever than that. Sometimes what you really need is a better rationalization for keeping useless stuff. Then it's not clutter anymore. It's "historic preservation" or something else equally worthy of respect.

Back to music. I'm on an e-mail list for music fans called Ecto. (This is a list for people who enjoy a particular kind of pop music; more at www.ecto.org.) I thought that with my seven-hundred-plus CDs, hundred-plus LPs, and hundred-plus cassette tapes, I had a real clutter problem. Then I met people on Ecto who have more than two thousand CDs: Many of these outwitting music clutter tips come from the Ecto list.

First, let me suggest something *not* to do: If you own more than a dozen CDs, don't try to organize them all alphabetically. There are several good reasons for this prohibition. Let's say that after sixteen hours you manage to get all your CDs arranged from A to Z. But have you? There's always going to be at least one CD that's out of order and *you will never, never, find that CD again.* Also, just because you were able to organize your CDs from ABBA to Zydeco Playboys (or is that under "Playboys, Zydeco"?) doesn't mean that you'll be able to maintain that organization. Every time you pull out a CD, you have to put it back in the same spot. And if you take out several at a time, your after-listening task becomes more time consuming. Human nature being what it is, most people are not inclined to put back a CD for every one they take out: Many people—maybe you—leave the organizing to later.

The other reason that alphabetizing isn't such a hot idea is that it makes it harder to expand your CD collection. If you buy a bunch of G's and M's, you have to start moving other CDs around to make room. It will be harder than you think (are you good at Rubik's cube?)

For a similar reason, it's not a wise idea to neatly stack all your CDs on a shelf or CD rack. Without room to expand, you will soon find yourself growing a CD tower alongside the shelf. This is especially dangerous if your household contains a tower-toppling toddler (and try saying that one, three times fast).

If your CDs are too well organized, you might become reluctant to use them, for fear of spoiling that order. (Don't scoff. I've seen it happen!)

Too precisely organized former clutter is nearly as bad as plain clutter.

Fortunately, there are numerous alternatives when it comes to organizing your music collection. I know I've mentioned this more than once in this book but it's a point that bears repeating: Many of the techniques you read about for one particular kind of clutter—say, music CDs—work for outwitting other kinds of clutter, too.

For projects like CDs, for which there may be dozens and dozens of individual objects, I suggest a modified group organizing system. What I mean by that is, organize your CDs by category: pop, rock, classical, hip-hop, jazz, and so on. That's the system I use and it works pretty well. For those categories of music for which I have too many CDs, I subdivide the category in alphabetical regions. For example, I have a lot of rock and roll CDs. Rather than just bunch them together, which would be a large group, I've broken down the rock CDs this way: rock, first quarter of the alphabet (A–F); second quarter (G–L); third quarter (M–R); and fourth quarter (S–Z, with more letters than the other groupings, because there aren't any X's and there are very few Y's and Z's). Within these quarters, I don't bother to alphabetize. That is to say, I'll put my Who CDs anywhere on the "Rock S–Z" shelf, not just in the W's.

One exception: Because I have more than a few Beatles CDs, I have a separate shelf just for Beatles CDs. This makes reshelving my CDs easy as pie, which is, after all, the whole point: An organizing system is worthless if you can't keep it up.

As you read this you may be thinking to yourself, "Hey, that's a great idea, but where the heck does he *put* all the CDs? That's my real problem."

That's a fair enough question: Obviously, I'm not storing my CDs in a temporal way station. And for many people—me included—that's the *big* problem. I used to keep my CDs in two giant CD swivel racks, each of which held three hundred CDs. They were kind of like lazy Susans for CDs. That system was all right, except for three problems. The CD racks were ugly. The racks took up too much space in my home office. And the CD slots went down to the floor, which meant that I had to get on my knees in order to find certain CDs, which meant that I never listened to those CDs. I really loathed getting down on the floor to locate particular tunes. Also, every time I did that I realized that I have a big dust-bunny problem in my office. For me, dust bunnies not seen are dust bunnies that don't exist. The CD rack system interfered with my perception of dust reality. You can see why I was looking for another storage option.

So I started thinking about some alternatives. I laid out my criteria: I wanted racks that were more attractive than the swivel things. I wanted them to be narrower, to take up less floor space. And most importantly, I wanted them not to go down to the floor where I'd have to squat among the dust bunnies that otherwise wouldn't exist in my consciousness. It was at this point that I had an epiphany. I suddenly understood that by coping with clutter you gain insight into what is truly important in your life. You discover certain planes of reality that you didn't know existed. You can choose to explore those planes or you can choose another path. That's what I did with the dust bunnies: I chose another way. From now on, I decreed, all CDs must be at knee level or higher. The best CDs should be at eye level. The least-frequently-listened-to should be an arm's reach up onto the higher shelves. By reorganizing along this general principle, I forced myself to consider which types of music I wanted close at hand, and which could be banished to remoter regions of space.

I still had to figure out what sort of storage system would give me flexibility to arrange my CDs at varying heights. The answer: bookshelves. Ordinary, cheap, particleboard, do-it-yourself IKEA bookshelves. No more specialized CD tray systems or swivel racks for me. From now on I would just line them up along the shelves, reserving the lowest two shelves for large, seldom-consulted books. My IKEA shelves are very adjustable as to height, so that I don't have much wasted space between shelves. I get about sixty CDs per fully loaded shelf. Many shelves are only two-thirds or three-quarters full; I use bookends to hold the CDs in place. That gives me plenty of room to expand within the subcategory on that particular shelf.

The beauty of the solution was that I already had the book-shelves in place in my home office. The trouble was, they were full of books—hundreds and hundreds of them that I'd acquired over the years. But I realized this: Except for the book I'm reading at any given moment, I don't consult my books very often. In fact, as more and more reference material gets put on the Internet and DVDs, I rarely open a paper dictionary, encyclopedia, almanac, or other reference book. Then there are my old college texts. *Essence of Decision: The Cuban Missile Crisis* is not a book that I'm going to need to have handy much these days. It took me only a couple of minutes to identify more than a hundred books that I could easily box up and put in storage in the basement, or else give away to someone who might actually look at them one day. Those hundred-plus books occupied more than twenty feet of bookshelf space—more than enough room to fit all my CDs.

I recognize, however, that my bookshelf solution is not for everyone. I consulted some other CD collectors and found some other solutions you might prefer. Neile Graham of Seattle, Washington, recommends the rack system:

> My CDs live in two storage towers, of a revolving type. As for the way the CDs are organized, at first I used to have one tower devoted to Australian CDs, the other holding "the rest of the world." I used to take pride in the fact they both held about an equal number of CDs! Then I tried to rearrange my collection by "type"; acoustic numbers together, electronics somewhere else, Natalie Merchant next to the Maniacs and Innocence Mission. Sarah Slean near Tori Amos . . . you get the idea. But soon I found things were too hard to find this way, since not every choice is clear-cut enough, and I'd often change my

mind as to where any particular CD should belong. In the end I settled for boring alphabetical order, leaving bits of space on each rack for additions. That worked well enough, until I started to run out of room!

My towers are getting pretty full and the obvious solution would be to buy a third tower, except I don't really have any space I could fit it in. So for now I limit the number of CDs instead, trying to keep it constant. As I get more CDs, I find some others I can discard. Those I just throw into the "discard pile" in the depths of my cupboard. Unfortunately those "depths" are getting pretty shallow too, and I guess I'll have to start selling some disks eventually. . . .

There are other, more inventive solutions to the CD storage problem. Here's how one music fan, Carolyn Andre, organizes her vast collection:

The bulk of them are in a slightly restructured closet. My house is a 1930s bungalow, and this particular variation of the design has a closet from the front bedroom which has a small stained-glass window on the rear wall, over the front porch. Since I had converted that room to be my "book/TV/music" room, it seemed extra foolish to close a closet door on a lovely window, so I removed the door and put in shelves along both side walls of the closet. The latch side (deeper recess) has some of those wall standard-type bookshelves. On the hinge side (shallower recess), I've been mounting five-inch by four-inch footboards on the wall with L brackets. If I recall, each board holds 150 to 200 CDs. The top shelf is classical and jazz, the bottom board is compilations and things like "best movie songs of. . . ."

The five shelves in between contain everything else, alphabetized by band/musician.

Carolyn also says that not all her CDs make it into the closet system: "And then there are the two cardboard file boxes containing various CDs I started to alphabetize but have not yet made it onto new boards. And several small stacks on top of one record cabinet—recent listening on the 'real' CD player. Then there are a few misplaced CDs on the dining room table—ones that wandered off to the day job listening for a while. Then we get into the bedroom that is now a computer-and-miscellaneous-files room. Six stacks of at least twenty-five CDs each on a wall shelf, an additional seven stacks encroaching on the computer desk, poised to spill over the printer paper tray—a few interspersed with Zip discs on top of the computer."

A few comments are in order. Carolyn's system, while neither perfect nor complete, works for her. Most importantly, this system is far better than no system at all. Not all of her CDs are in Carolyn's music closet, but most of them are. You don't have to completely and thoroughly outwit clutter each and every time. You can gnaw away at clutter, too.

Although I personally think it's a bad idea to alphabetize your CDs, not everyone agrees. (They'll be sorry!) But if you do decide to put your CDs in alphabetical order, here's one suggestion, which comes from Phil Hudson:

> Here's an interesting way to organize large numbers of CDs that doesn't require you to rearrange everything whenever you buy new ones:
>
> First alphabetize everything in your collection.
>
> Now number them all, starting with the number 10 and adding 5 for each CD (10, 15, 20, 25, and so on). If

you intend to collect a lot of a particular artist's works, leave a few more numbers available in that range.

Now create your master list and alphabetize that to figure out where they all are! This way, as you add more CDs, you don't need to renumber or rearrange the whole collection, you simply add 21 or 36 or whatever. As long as you keep your numbering together, and maintain the master list, it works. Of course, if you buy *lots* of CDs and run out of numbers too soon, then you're in trouble.

TWO TIPS FOR OUTWITTING MUSIC CLUTTER

Problem 1: Vinyl LP albums that you rarely or never play.

Solution: Replace them with CDs or have them converted to CDs.

Problem 2: Too many CDs.

Solution: Take them out of their jewel boxes and put them in CD sleeves.

Your Keys

Raise your hand if you have *never* lost your keys.

I'm confident that *no hands* will go up in response to that. Why? Because we are disorganized when it comes to our keys, mostly because we can't find them amidst all the other clutter that's around.

A lot of people have suggested that you set aside a single place for your keys and only leave them in that spot. This way, you'll always know where your keys are. Sounds good in theory, but it fails the basic reality test. Anybody who can always leave the keys in the same place probably doesn't have a clutter problem, or leads an awfully slow-paced life. Haven't you ever come in the front door to your house and had to dash to answer the phone? The keys get plopped down near the telephone. Or have you had to rush inside to change your child's diaper because it's, er, leaking? You might accidentally put your house keys in the box of wipes. (You hope you didn't drop them in the diaper pail!) Or what about when you're so thoroughly exhausted that you just leave your keys in your coat or pant pocket?

Still, it helps to have a designated spot for house keys just so that you know which place to search first when you're running late to a meeting. A hook by the door is a likely spot to leave them each time you return home. If you think keys dangling from hooks look ugly, then consider a decorative box with a flip-up lid.

Whatever spot you choose, if you have a toddler, make sure it's out of your child's reach. You want to avoid what happened to this New Jersey mother: "I remember one time my two-year-old son had taken the keys and put them in a gopher hole out in the backyard. We didn't find them for a very long time."

Catalogs

Despite the Internet, paper catalogs still arrive in the mail. And nobody's really complaining about them, either, because catalogs are so much fun to browse through. It's like window-shopping; thumbing through a glossy catalog while lying in bed is far more enjoyable than using the "Page Down" button to do the same sort of thing in front of your computer screen.

But catalogs take up space. They collect dust. They quickly become clutter.

So throw them out.

It's that simple. If you're not planning to order from a catalog right away, you don't need to keep it. And if for some reason you discover that you did want to order from a catalog you now longer have, I *guarantee* that you'll find *exactly* what you're looking for on the Internet. Catalogs are fun but they're absolutely disposable; there's no reason on earth that they should cause you clutter pain.

By the way, catalogs make great bathroom reading before they hit the trash can.

Hair Stuff

I have to say that I don't usually think much about hair. Here's why:

This is me.

But here is another member of my family:

As you can see, there's a fair amount disparity in the hair department. Before I got married and had kids, I never really thought much about hair. But in some ways that gave me an advantage when it came to outwitting hair clutter. You may already know this, but I discovered, as my kids grew older and their hair grew longer, that lots of hair requires lots of brushes (one brush won't do, definitely not), combs, bobby pins, scrunchies, ponytail holders, barrettes, hair bands, ribbons, and lots and lots of other little clippie things that may have names, but I don't know what they are. Well, clutter, that's what they are.

And as clutter, they can be tamed (if I didn't have confidence in that, I wouldn't be writing this book). My first taming impulse was to decree that it was up to the owner of the hair to keep all her cluttery hair things out of my way. But with two daughters, both of whom have a lot of hair, that didn't work; all it led to was this perpetual refrain: "That's not *my* hair band—it's hers!"

Rather than be saddled with the impossible task of learning whose tiny clips were whose, I realized I had to take a different tack. Collective responsibility. Collectivization of the hair supplies. Centralization, leading to strong-arm control—a technique the Stalinists used to subdue the starving peasant masses in the 1930s. I decreed henceforth that all stray hair supplies would be thrown into a central location, where they would no longer have individual owners but could be used by anyone with hair. The kitchen was a fine location, far from either child's bedroom. So was born "the hair drawer."

I set aside a smallish drawer, threw out all the matches and toothpicks and cocktail napkins that had been taking up space before, and immediately refilled it with the various brushes and hair ornaments I gathered up from around the house. The very next morning as the girls were finishing up their breakfast and getting ready to go to school, my wife said, "Each of you, go

back upstairs and brush your hair. You can't go to school looking like that."

"Wait," I said, grinning at my own cleverness. "No need to go
anywhere. The brushes are right here in this drawer. And so are
all the hair ties."

I had made it impossible for either child to procrastinate by
going back upstairs and claiming to be unable to find the brush
or hair thing she wanted. It was all there!

The hair drawer is something we have maintained for hair-
dressing efficiency ever since—one of my most successful outwitting clutter inventions.

Wallets and Purses

Lots of clutter ends up in people's wallets and purses. Let me
talk about wallets first, because I'm a guy and I really have no
idea of what goes inside a woman's purse. While wallets are
small and compact, they attract their fair share of clutter,
too. Mostly this clutter is in the form of receipts and expired
credit and membership cards, and while the paper receipts
don't take up much room, the credit cards can pile up. At
one-sixteenth of an inch thick, a single credit card doesn't
seem like much, but pile ten of them together and you've got
a hefty stack that can become a menace to your back. Believe
it or not (when I use that phrase, I actually mean "it's true"),
too-thick wallets have been shown to put weight where it
doesn't belong, contributing to disc pressure on the nerves
in the spine.

The solution: Simple enough—take out any cards you don't
use on a regular basis. Do you need to always carry three gasoline company cards with you when you take the subway to the
office? Do you need to take your office credit card or office ID

with you on vacation? Do you need a library card when you travel out of town?

The fewer credit cards you carry, the less mayhem there will be in your life if your wallet is ever borrowed by somebody who neglects to ask permission (that is, if you're pickpocketed). If you always have every single credit and identification card, when your wallet is lost or stolen, you've got nothing. Conversely, if you do keep a few cards at home, then you've got a buffer should anything happen to your wallet.

When you have a few moments, take *everything* out of your wallet. (This is best *not* done in a public place, such as a doctor's waiting room or a bus station.) Before you put anything back, ask yourself if you really need it. Get rid of any pictures of your children that are more than a few years old. Those pictures of your ex-girlfriend should definitely go. Receipts, bank deposit slips, thirty-two-cent postage stamps—all that can go. (The adhesive on the back of those old stamps is dead, isn't it? Even if it isn't, do you really want to lick it?) When you're finished, you have a leaner, meaner wallet, and you won't look as though you're carrying a paperback novel in your back pant pocket.

Do this every few months. Decluttering a wallet is probably one of the least difficult things you can do as far as clutter is involved, because it requires very little physical effort, and success can be measured in inches or centimeters, not by the roomful.

On to purses. I'm not willing to go out on a limb and say what a woman needs or doesn't need in her handbag. That's dangerous territory for a guy. But I am willing to say that almost every time my wife has asked me to get something that's "in my purse," I haven't been able to find it. Worse, I've been fearful that there's something in the bag that's going to bite my fingers off. Of course that fear is completely unfounded, but the part about never being able to find anything in my wife's bag is absolutely true. (Actually, there is one thing that I can find and that's the miniature flashlight I put in her bag a year ago. She still hasn't noticed that it's in there. There's a lesson here somewhere.)

Car Clutter

A friend of mine keeps the neatest apartment I've ever been in. His few pieces of furniture are spare, minimalist, and with hardly anything interrupting the clean flow of lines. Clutter doesn't stand a chance there. His car, on the other hand, is another matter entirely. *Messy* doesn't cover it; *disgusting* might come close. The one time I rode in it, I had the horrible feeling that my pants might stick to the seat and my shoes might adhere to the floor. Ever since that time I've always been quick to volunteer to drive whenever we've made plans to do something together.

I've been good about keeping my car in shape so that I can offer a ride to someone on the spur of the moment, without having to apologize or move lots of stuff to the trunk.

Wouldn't it be great if you had a convertible and could simply turn your car upside down and shake out all the junk that's accumulated?

That would be a fast way of dealing with the clutter and mess inside your car. Since you can't do that, you might think the solution is to keep a trash bag in your car. That's what most people do. But in fact, the trash bag idea is a bad one, and rarely works. If you own one of those little car trash bags that strap onto the back of the headrest, I'm sure you've discovered how quickly the bag fills up. And worse: It fills up with gooey, ucky stuff and you feel compelled to either throw the bag out after you've used it just once, or never touch the bag again, which amounts to the

same thing. Alternatively, some people use little plastic super-
market bags as trash bags, but once these bags fill up and are
tossed out, the tendency is not to replace them.

No, my friends, all ordinary ways of dealing with car mess
don't work.

What you need to do is to first think about the kinds of clutter in your car. (I hope by now that you've come to realize that
this book is a *thinking person's* book. No coasting.) There are two
kinds of car clutter: garbage and stuff. Let's talk a little more
about garbage first. Some people have a rule that nobody's allowed to eat in their car, ever, and that goes a long way toward
keeping the inside of a car neat and clean. These people, by the
way, are called single people. Families are much harder to control. Babies are impossible. When they're hungry, they've got to
have something—a bottle, a handful of Cheerios, something—
whether they're in the car or not. But where there is food, there
will be garbage. It's that simple.

Since a trash bag doesn't really work, you need another system for getting the garbage out of your car, and here it is: Just
put trash in your pockets. I'm not kidding. It's a great way to
outwit trash. A little removed from your car every day will start
you on the road toward a cleaner car. I can also promise that
you're not likely to keep any gum wrappers, doughnut bags,
and coffee twirlers in your pockets for long.

But food trash is the lesser part of the car clutter problem.
The bigger problem for most people is the stuff they intention-
ally keep in their cars—stuff they really don't need to have
there. About this, *Boston Globe* columnist Ellen Goodman once
remarked that when she sold her car, she felt she was moving
out of it. It's not just the maps, flashlights, umbrellas, blankets,
folding chairs, flares, extra sneakers, paperback novels (for the
passenger), CDs, tapes, sunglasses, small camping stoves, old

road atlases, water bottles, clothes to be returned, McDonald's toys, computer discs, and extra batteries. It's that all this stuff has no other place to go, or so it seems. It feels as if these things belong in our cars. But the truth is that clutter makes driving less enjoyable, just as clutter makes everything else in life less fun. It's also dangerous. If you stop short, the clutter can fly all over the place.

And that doesn't even include what's lurking in your trunk and glove compartment. (I bet you're afraid to open your glove compartment, for fear of not being able to close it again.)

Decluttering a car requires brute force—there's no trick, no magic, no special system you can use. You simply have to go through your car, item by item, and clean it out. Fortunately, much of what's in your car is stuff that you can simply throw away without having to worry about where to put it, including broken umbrellas, old maps, old registration and insurance information, and cassettes you never listen to anymore. That's the first thing you should do—get rid of the old, tired, broken things. Chances are that after you're done, you'll have a car with 50 percent less clutter.

Next, take a look at the duplicated things in your car: Many people have several maps of the same place, for instance. You don't need more than one flashlight, as long as you periodically check to be sure that the batteries in it are still good. Remove what you don't need an extra of.

There are two very different but effective ways of dealing with the clutter that remains after your big car cleanout:

1. You can buy car-organizer-type products from an auto-supply store or from a hardware store and use them to keep your car things neat. To give you an idea of what's out there: You can buy attach-to-the-visor CD organizers;

extra cup holders that hang from the inside edges of your windows; coin sorters; over-the-seat map holders; backseat car trays with storage space underneath the tray; and a wide assortment of add-on pockets and cases for all kinds of things.

2. You can buy a new car. Sure, it's an extreme solution, but I know people who have done it. That's right, the only solution they could find to their car clutter problem was to trade their old station wagon for a new monster version of an SUV. You know the kind I'm talking about—twenty-seven different cup holders, fifty-two separate compartments, enough cargo room to haul a year's supply of diapers for septuplets, a stereo/VCR/DVD system wired so that six backseat passengers can all watch or listen to different channels, a roof rack for both skis and bikes, and enough horsepower to tow a small asteroid. Keep in mind, however, that within six months, even this huge vehicle could well be cluttered up, unless the owners practice preventive decluttering (see chapter 8).

6

Office Clutter

Starting from Scratch

What's it like to have an uncluttered desk? Try this experiment.
Remove virtually everything from your desk. Just put it in a cardboard box, or stuff everything away in a closet for the time
being. Don't worry about doing a meaningful declutter; the ob-
jective here is to see what your desk looks like with nothing on
it. (Or just a pen, a telephone, and a photo of your golden re-
triever.) Leave it that way for a day or two. Resist the temptation
to return something you "need" to your desk. Now try to go
back to the old ways of a cluttered desk. I bet you won't. Once
you've had a taste of a clean, uncluttered desk, you'll want to
keep it that way.

And you can.

Below are some ideas that can help.

The In-Box System

Preferred by movie set designers, the In-Box System is straightforward and uncomplicated. You have a stacker on your desk
with an in-box and an out-box. Into the in-box goes all the stuff

that you have to work on; in the out-box goes all the stuff that you've completed and is just waiting to be mailed and/or filed. Sounds simple and easy to maintain, right?

Well, not for everyone, myself among them. I tried this system once and here's what happened: My in-box wasn't big enough. Not even close. There were six inches between my in-box and my out-box and in about two weeks I had at least seven inches of stuff in my in-box, which meant that my out-box was now off its frame and resting on a pile of paper. Not only that, but there was no organization to my in-box at all—it was just a stack of paper. Mail mixed with bills, mixed with photos needing to be framed, mixed with government forms, mixed with a letter from a fan, mixed with a couple of magazine articles I clipped, mixed with printouts from the Internet, mixed with lots of other stuff. (Why I thought it was necessary to print pages from the Internet is another saga—anything from the Internet is best saved on a computer, not printed out, which instantly converts it to clutter.)

Not a very good system, at least for me. For plenty of other people the In-Box System works very well, but for a lot of us—I hesitate to say "most of us"—this method works for exactly one week. Then all-powerful clutter takes over again.

Clutter is so sly that you have to be careful of letting the In-Box System stick around longer than you want it to. Once you've decided that a system of in-boxes and out-boxes doesn't work for you, *get rid of your in-box/out-box*. It's counterproductive to leave the stacker on your desk, unless you want to have a reminder of clutter's power and craftiness.

THE IN-BOX SYSTEM

Pro: Simple, easy-to-set-up system.

Con: Can easily turn into a pile of paper.

If the simple in-box/out-box method doesn't work for you, there is a way to modify it so that it will be useful to you in your battle against clutter. But this variation requires that you make a deal with the clutter devil. Here's what I mean: Get a really big box, or a gigantic salad bowl, or some other out-sized container to hold your mountain of papers. Just make that entire container your in-box. When paper comes in that you can't figure out what to do with, just put it in your big new bin of an in-box.

I have to admit that this is what I do. My wife and I received a beautiful but enormous zebra-wood bowl as a wedding present. It was way too big for a salad bowl (unless someday we decide to make salad for everyone in Grand Central Station). We didn't have a kitchen cabinet deep enough to hold it. It was even too big to fit comfortably on our narrow dining room table. We graciously thanked the giver, but for years wondered where to put it, and doubted that we would ever use it. Then one day it hit me: I could bring it to my office and finally have something big enough for all the things that won't fit in my in-box. And it's quite an attractive thing, to boot. Now all the stuff that can't be thrown away or dealt with right away goes straight into that bowl. About every four months I turn the bowl upside down and rummage through the papers. About 90 percent of what's in my so-called in-box gets discarded at that point, though, in truth, there are a few items—no more than half an inch worth—that have stayed in my in-box bowl since I came up with idea nearly three years ago.

The "Touched-Paper" Rule

You may have heard this bit of business wisdom: Once you touch a piece of paper, you must do something with it:

- Act on it.
- File it.
- Throw it away.

This saying implies that a major source of clutter is *not* following this rule, because *not* doing something about each and every piece of paper means that the paper will just hang around.

I'm here to tell you that the rule is wrong. You don't have to immediately do something with everything. Don't misunderstand; I'm not suggesting that this is a bad policy; it's good in concept. But if you make this maxim your mantra and feel that you must always, absolutely, unconditionally do something with every piece of paper you touch, you'll put yourself into a rigid box, stifle your own creativity, and drive yourself nuts. And if you don't drive yourself nuts, you will drive people around you nuts.

There should be no fixed, unbending rules when it comes to dealing with clutter. When you outwit clutter, you're being smart. It's not smart to stick to a single rule under all circumstances.

Let's examine this touched-paper rule a bit more closely. This rule dictates that you need to take action on the paper you're holding in your hand or throw that paper out. But how realistic is that? Let's say you get a query from the Internal Revenue Service, or perhaps a fan letter: According to this rule, you need to do something about those letters immediately or throw them away. But if you're not prepared to take action on the IRS letter right now (because your accountant is on vacation) and you throw it away, the IRS is going to sic its agents on you. Throw away the fan letter (because you get so many that you can no longer respond to every one right away) and the fan might turn out to be a stalker, and now your first piece of evidence is gone. Hard to say which is worse, though neither is desirable. In either event, you need time to respond judiciously. You *should* procrastinate, in other words. Wait until your accountant or, better still, your lawyer, has had time to look at that IRS letter and tell you what it means. Maybe you *can* toss it without a worry (fat chance!). Maybe you'll conclude, now that you're such a big star, that you need to hire a secretary to handle your fan mail for you. These kinds of decisions can't be made on the spur of the moment.

So it goes with much of the paper you receive: It has to be dealt with later.

It would be great if we all had assistants to deal with our incoming clutter-to-be, but that's not the case. So we have to figure out where to put all those papers that we can't or won't take care of immediately.

The best system is the one that works for you and that doesn't create clutter. There's no one-size-fits-all solution for me to recommend. You need a method of organizing your incoming paper that is customized for you. For some people, a simple in-box works; for others, a more complicated in-box, divided into subsections: "Urgent," "Important," and "When Time Permits." Some brave souls devote a corner of their desk to their incoming mail and memos.

There's one important factor that you should consider when setting up your paper-coping system: your memory. What's the best way to keep yourself from forgetting about what's in that mountain of paper that will probably pile up, when things get really busy at work? For a few people, it's enough to have the paper physically sitting in the in-box. But most of us, given a busy schedule, will end up regarding the in-box pile as "invisible clutter"—a concept I've already discussed in reference to the piles of stuff you no longer notice around your house. So in addition to setting up a physical place to put your paper clutter, you need to devise a means of reminding yourself to deal with it by each paper's deadline.

If you use paper reminders, such as Post-it notes, you have to worry about the pileup of paper reminders becoming yet another layer of ignored clutter. That's why I prefer electronic reminders. I keep an electronic calendar on my computer that chimes gently as the deadlines for dealing with various bits of paperwork loom. Right now I can scan the month to come and see that I need to fill out some tax forms by the fifteenth of the month, pay my bills by the end of the month, obtain permission from the author to use an e-mail decluttering tip I've included in an earlier chapter of this book, and get the completed manuscript in to the publisher in less than two weeks (yikes!). I like the electronic calendar I use because whenever a reminder pops up on my screen, it asks me whether I want to: push the deadline back to some other date, ask to be reminded later on for the same deadline, or mark the task as done and dismiss all further reminders. I won't tell you which button I click on most frequently.

Whatever system you use, whether for piling up the papers or for reminding yourself that they still exist, you should ensure that it meets three basic criteria:

1. It's easy for you to understand and put into practice.
2. It tames clutter rather than spreads it.
3. It keeps you from losing important things (that is to say, it works).

OUTWITTING CLUTTER TIP

Keep your trash can close to your desk.

If the trash can is on the other side of your office, you'll be less inclined to use it. However, if you've turned your trash can into a basketball hoop, and you miss, use the opportunity to get some exercise by running after the "ball" and shooting until you score.

Fax Away Your Paper Piles

Paper is the bane of those of us who want to tame our clutter. Paper just piles up, and yet we often can't throw out individual pieces of paper because what's on the paper is important, such as driving directions to our child's team's opening game, a vacation itinerary, troubleshooting instructions for a computer product, or access codes to our online banking service. And so the paper just sits there, useful, but the center of the clutter universe.

Fortunately, there's more than one way to skin a pineapple. (Well, actually, I have no idea if there's more than one way or not, but it sounds right and allows me to avoid that gory cliché about skinning a cat.) Fax the paper to your e-mail address. Then store the information just as you would save any other piece of e-mail. I use a free electronic fax service called eFax (www.efax.com), but there are others, such as J2.com, that offer differing levels of communications services for a monthly fee. You're assigned a fax number and provided with software to download that converts your incoming faxes to a form that you can read on your computer and store electronically, or print out, if you are so inclined. It's a very convenient way to manage an overflow of paper. These services also let you convert your faxes into graphics files, so you can store the information in a variety of formats, though that capability may be more than you want.

Alternatively, you could purchase a scanner with a paper feeder, but those devices are pretty expensive. If you already have a stand-alone fax machine, faxing paper to yourself lets you take advantage of equipment you already own.

Now for the most important component of this advice: *After you have stored the information electronically, throw that piece of paper out!*

Return Trip Trouble

Dear Clutter Adviser:

I have train tickets that need to be returned for a credit, because we never used them. (We actually caught an earlier train from New York to Boston.) I called Amtrak and they said that I could send the tickets back for a refund, but I don't trust sending four hundred dollars' worth of train tickets through the mail. So eventually I plan to bring them to Penn Station and get a refund in person. Only I haven't yet. The tickets are sitting here on my desk. I'm afraid to put these train tickets in a drawer because then I might forget about them entirely. I don't want them on my desk, either, but I really don't have a choice. Or do I?

Signed,

RR Man

Dear RR:

Send the tickets back in the mail and take your chances. Or take no chances, and send them registered and insured. Otherwise, it sounds as if you'll delay and delay until a convenient time comes around, and then you'll discover that the last day you were allowed to exchange them was yesterday.

As a general rule, if you can do something today by mail or e-mail, do it that way. Laziness and procrastination are the evil kin of clutter, but any service that will pick things up from your door and deliver them to someone else can become your ally in the war against clutter.

PIM to the Rescue!

PIM is short for "personal information manager." The beauty of using a PIM as a decluttering tool is that a PIM has nearly an infinite number of applications.

I can hear you thinking, "Why should I buy a new thing?—it might just become more clutter." Well, because if you already own a personal computer, the odds are you already have a PIM that came with the "bundle" of programming installed on your hard drive from the start. All you probably need to do is start making use of the asset you have. PIMs typically store several different categories of information:

- Contacts (otherwise know as names and addresses).
- Calendar.
- Notes.
- To-do list.
- Expenses.

In addition to PC programs that handle the above functions, there's also a wide variety of handheld devices that run PIM programs. If you have a PDA (that is, a personal digital assistant, otherwise known as a Palm Pilot, Pocket PC, Rex, BlackBerry, or some other brand of handheld computer)—then you definitely have personal information manager software.

Some people have experience with a variant on the PIM—the loose-leaf paper version, very popular in the 1980s under the name Filofax or Day Runner. It was a combination address book, calendar, expense-account recorder, and more.

So how do you use a PIM as an anticlutter device? Just expand your imagination to think of uses beyond the few it was designed to handle. Think laterally. Think creatively. Use your originality. Or just read the next few paragraphs.

Why not use your PIM to remember where you put things away? If you regularly keep information in your PIM's contacts compartment, you'll never have to run around the house frantically searching for that "safe place" where you put the thing away. For instance, we have an American flag that we display on appropriate occasions, such as Veterans Day and Flag Day. Because we don't put the flag up all that often, we keep it in one of those safe places, which for us is a basement closet. To remember where we're storing the flag, all I have to do is look up "flag" in my PIM. With a two-character keystroke, "Control F," I pull up the "Find" menu, type in "flag," and my computer whirs for a tenth of a second and then spits out the answer, "In the basement closet."

The alternative is to keep the flag in a prominent place, such as the front hall closet, where it would contribute to the closet's clutter. We keep track of a variety of seldom-used things in a PIM, including the car snow scraper, swim goggles, passports, holiday lights, yellow-jacket traps, next year's calendar, and a photograph trimmer. Without using a PIM we'd have much less latitude when it comes to choosing where to store something.

You can also make creative use of the calendar in your PIM. Again, rather than keeping something out on a desk or counter, put an alarm bell in your PIM's calendar for that date. Our neighborhood movie theater sold advance tickets for *Harry Potter and the Sorcerer's Stone*. We didn't want to forget where these tickets were, but we didn't want to leave them on our front hall table for two weeks, either. So I noted in the calendar entry for the 11:30 A.M. showing of *Harry Potter* that the movie tickets were in the left-hand drawer in my desk. By noting the location of the tickets along with the calendar information, I turned what would have been temporary clutter into no clutter at all. A couple of hours before the movie was due to start, my PIM went "ding-dong" and a window popped up saying, "Remember Harry Potter tix in left-hand desk drawer."

Another unexpected use to make of your PIM is the "Notes" feature of most programs. In "Notes" you can keep paperless versions of things that would otherwise be scribbled down on real pieces of paper and possibly mislaid. If you're the sort of person who uses too many Post-it notes (see the section below to find out if you are), then you might prefer to get into the habit of making notes on your computer instead. On my program (it's Microsoft Outlook, and it has its pluses and minuses) I can make the background of the notes appear as a corkboard and the little squares of paper appear pinned there as if with pushpins. It's odd: The program allows you to create what looks just like a very cluttered bulletin board, if that's what you want. (I do try to keep mine neat.) What kind of notes do I write to myself in "Notes"? Anything I might otherwise have scribbled on the back of an envelope or on some other handy scrap of paper: ideas to remember for birthday presents, cooking tips, shopping lists, promises made by the customer service representative about the credit due on my account, things to remember to pack for an outing, names of restaurants someone has recommended, hours of the car inspection station, the inflation pressure on the kids' bike tires, their locker combinations, and anything else I have a sudden need to jot down. Occasionally, I transfer the information (usually by cut-and-paste method—it's much faster than retyping) into some other section of my PIM, such as the address book, the calendar, or the to-do list. Usually, though, I just use "Notes" for short-term things I felt like writing down but don't need to save in any special place. When I'm done with the note, I hit the "Delete" key, and it's gone. No scrap of paper turns up months later in illegible handwriting, leaving me to wonder, "What was this all about—and do I need to save it?"

The address book feature is another part of the PIM I've learned to use in ways beyond the mere storage of names, addresses, and telephone numbers. For example, my younger daughter Claire has a friend who lives on a street that's very hard to find. The first few times I went to drop Claire off at her friend's house, I took along directions, as well as the address. I never could remember where I put those directions, so I had to call the parents each time to get the information all over again. They must have thought I was disorganized! But then it occurred to me that I could store the directions in the address book section of my PIM. Then, whenever I clicked on that name, the directions would pop up along with the address and phone number. I never had to search for a piece of paper with written directions again, and better still, never had to make that embarrassing phone call to ask for directions again.

Once you get into the habit of putting nontraditional information in your PIM, you'll remember that's where the information is.

Post-it Notes: Boon or Bane?

Before 1980 there were no Post-it notes, therefore no Post-it notes clutter. After Spencer Silver's invention was brought to market by the 3M Corporation, an organizing tool was born, but so was a problem. Like the proverbial double-edged sword, Post-it notes can serve as a weapon in the war against clutter, but when misused can make the situation worse than it ever was before.

They're probably easier to misuse than use with proper restraint, so let's start with the danger first: You write far too many things down on Post-it notes, and after scribbling each note, you stick it to something. Time passes, and you either act on what you've written down and then forget to remove the note, or you don't act on it and so leave the note up week after week, telling yourself, "I'll get to it later." Either way, you have notes stuck to things all around you. Then there's a third source of Post-it note clutter: the notes you stuck onto something that fell down once the barely sticky adhesive backing became dusty and landed on something else, covering it up, or—worse—landed under something else, and you don't see the reminder until it's long past time to act on what the note was supposed to have reminded you to do. If this is what you're doing, then Post-it notes are a bane, and there's only one solution for you: Give them up!

On the other hand, if you are someone who uses Post-it notes judiciously (or you can train yourself to use them judiciously), then you will probably find them a boon. You use them to:

- Mark pages in catalogs and books. You discard them the minute you've ordered from the catalog or finished the book in question.

- Take phone messages at telephones that do not have a specific telephone message pad with lined spaces to record time, date, "for," "from," and "concerning." If you use Post-it notes for phone messages, you must take care to transfer the note without delay to wherever its intended recipient would be most likely to see it.

- Write reminders to yourself, once you have worked out a practical system for keeping those reminders in a specific place, reviewing them regularly, and tossing out the notes when you have completed the task.

- Make temporary labels for objects, photos, or papers that you do not want marked by a permanent label. For example, if you organize your photographs by subject instead of by date, you might tack a Post-it to the back, letting it stick up like a tab, and on the tab write a subject label. You can then easily put all the photos in shoe boxes (or archival photo storage boxes) by subject.

You should *not* be using Post-it notes for any of the following:

- Writing drafts of letters. (That will take too many and will be too hard to keep in order.)
- Putting driving directions on them (unless they're so simple that you can easily fit them on a single Post-it note; otherwise you end up having to search for page two and page three while also looking at the road—very dangerous!).
- Any outdoor use, such as leaving instructions for delivery people or guests on your front door (the adhesive is not strong enough to keep them from blowing off in even the lightest wind).

Business Cards

Clutter isn't always composed of big things. Take business cards—they're not very big along any of their dimensions, and even a stack of business cards isn't going to take up that much room. So what's the big deal? Why clutter up part of this book with information about organizing business cards?

The answer is that if you can't control the little things, what hope do you have of dealing with the bigger, meaner stuff when it comes along? (Okay, that wasn't an answer, but another question.) Getting a handle on the business cards you receive is good practice for working up to the hard stuff, like, let's say, business directories.

There are two or three different, easy methods that work. Simplest is to file them in a recipe box or an index-card file. Some people think boxes take up too much room and prefer a loose-leaf binder with special business-card-sized pocket pages. I personally go for disposing of the paper version altogether and saving only the information itself electronically (meaning that I retype all the phone numbers and addresses into my computer's address book program, unless I can get the person to e-mail me a card that I can simply drag into my electronic address book).

Any of these three systems is better than letting the cards lie around on your desk, in your briefcase, in your glove compartment, or in your pant pocket (where they'll undoubtedly end up at the dry cleaners on the day you absolutely must find that person's direct-dial number).

I view business cards as a microcosm of the clutter universe. I daresay that you can't outwit the rest of your office clutter unless you can outwit business card clutter. (But the converse, unfortunately, is not necessarily true: Outwitting business card clutter does not guarantee that you'll outwit the rest of your clutter.)

Office Clutter by the Dozen:
Twelve Common Types of Clutter to Reduce or Eliminate Altogether

An office is supposed to be a place of efficiency and productivity. All too often it is a place where things accumulate that interfere with both those goals. There's too much of this, too many of that. Here are some of the most common thises and thats of office clutter . . . and what to do about them.

Item	*Strategy*
1. Wires	Trace all wires to their source. Any wire not connected to an essential device should be weeded out. All wires running in more or less the same direction should be taped together or snaked through a single wire tube.

2. Pens and pencils	Keep out one black pen, one blue pen, one spare pen of the preferred color, plus two sharpened regular pencils, plus (optional) one red pencil. Objective: to fit all writing implements into one slim pencil cup.
3. Notepads	Most people only need one for notes and messages. If you like to write drafts in longhand, possibly keep a second larger pad for that purpose.
4. Calendars	If you need more than one, your calendar system needs rethinking.
5. Rulers, tape measures	Unless you're a contractor or tailor or some other professional who does lots of measuring, pick one measuring implement that works for you and borrow others only when you need them.
6. Staplers, staple removers, hole punchers	Keep one stapler with a staple remover next to it. If you find yourself punching holes on a regular basis, then keep a hole puncher handy—one- or three-hole, whichever you prefer, but not both.
7. Rolls of tape	Keep one regular roll in a refillable dispenser. Stow other tapes (double-stick, strapping, masking) unless used daily.
8. Paper clips, alligator clips, butterfly clips, and other fasteners	Pick one type for small packets of papers, one other type for larger packets, and find a double-compartment container to hold a handy quantity of each.

9. Scissors, box cutters, letter openers, clippers	Look for a multitool with blades for all the cutting jobs in your office. Buy a small sharpener to keep it useful, so you won't be tempted to get new cutters.
10. Mailing supplies	Keep on hand just what you use frequently. Put all other mailing supplies away on shelves or in labeled bins.
11. Reference books	I say get rid of 'em all and get your information online!
12. Paperweights	I've never understood why anyone owns one. Is anyone's office so windy that papers actually blow away unless weighted?

Changing Your Office's Clutter Rules

Here's a story that may be an urban legend, but still has the ring of truth to it: From time to time the General Services Administration, a bureaucracy that functions as the office manager for all the other bureaucracies in the government, sends experts to various agencies to suggest ways to improve these agencies' efficiency and reduce waste.

A GSA expert suggested that the Federal Trade Commission reduce the amount of paper it stored by throwing out certain correspondence older than ten years. The FTC thought that was a good idea, but pointed out that it would have to make three copies of each letter first.

Sometimes—probably too often—you may be thwarted in your anticlutter campaign by what's commonly called

"Rules," but may be called "Procedures for Maintaining and Managing the Normal and Standard Operating System for the Organization." (Cluttered way of saying, "Rules.") The rules may make it impossible for you to clean out your filing cabinet, make space to put a single picture of your family on your desk, or dispose of Post-it notes once you've scribbled anything on them. If your anticlutter efforts encounter this kind of stumbling block, there are really only two things you can do about it: Find someplace else to put your clutter, or get the Procedures for Maintaining and Managing the Normal and Standard Operating System for the Organization (er, rules) changed.

For the first option, go through the tips in this book (not just in this chapter on office clutter) to find new techniques and approaches for all that clutter you're prohibited from throwing away.

For the second option, getting the rules changed, you'll have to talk to your boss. Go in with confidence and outline your plan as if it's some brilliant new business strategy that you just thought up on your own. On second thought, don't—individual initiative is all too often suspect in the corporate world. Better still, say you learned the technique in Jack Welch's mega-best-seller autobiography, *Jack: Straight from the Gut*. After all, he made his name as an industry legend by dumping thousands of excess employees who were obviously just cluttering up the place. Your office can surely do as much with the excess paper.

Oh, and here's a third option that just occurred to me if the problem is a rulebound workplace that won't let you declutter on your own. Quit! Get a better job or strike out on your own and become your own boss. An extreme solution, to be sure, but in some extreme cases, nothing less will do.

The End of the Workday

At the end of the workday, before you go home—or if you work at home, before you knock off until tomorrow—you should tidy up a bit. For some things, like offices, outwitting clutter is a daily process, and while it's okay to skip a day, if you don't tend to your physical space on a regular basis, clutter is going to overwhelm you.

So before the day is done:

- Tidy up your desk.
- Organize your notes into a single pile, or better still, transfer all your notes to your computer.
- Empty the trash if the can is overflowing.
- Put pens in their place.
- Clear out any surface that's been taken over by clutter. Chairs especially have a tendency to collect clutter and that single piece of mail left on your "guest chair" has the magical ability to multiply overnight, so that when you return in the morning, it's become a scary pile.
- If there's any equipment that needs more supplies, order those supplies now (but only as long as you have a set-aside place to keep them until they're needed).
- Anything that can be thrown out should be thrown out.

The Home Office

Everyone has a home office, even if it's just a part of the kitchen in which you organize and pay bills. The home office, be it makeshift or a dedicated room, is one of the places in a house that accumulates considerable clutter, which, like any clutter, needs to be dealt with. However, because a home office is different from the office where you're paid to do work, different strategies are necessary.

Of all the differences between home offices and downtown offices, the first and most critical is that a home office isn't cleaned every night by a janitorial staff. The dust in the corner of a home office stays in the corner until *you* decide to deal with it. Same thing with the trash can—nobody empties it on a daily basis.

Home offices also aren't governed by a set of rules dictated by higher-ups. (I bet you'd like to see *these people's* home offices, wouldn't you?) Many corporate offices have requirements about decor (the book publishing world, where stacks of manuscripts threaten to become fire hazards, excepted). These rules, which can range from requiring nothing pinned to the wall to only allowing pictures of the senior management's children on your desk, do help with curtailing clutter. But anticlutter rules, enforced under the penalty of termination, don't work at home. (They often don't even work when you try to enforce them on your kids!) Downtown offices are also designed to impress (should I say *intimidate?*) and so they have to present a certain solidity. Very few home offices, however, are set up in such a way as to imply, "My paycheck's bigger than your paycheck."

And so home offices fall into disarray. Pleasant, unobtrusive pieces of paper become piles of paper or, worse, become a kind of tablecloth for your desk. Books get squeezed into bookshelves so tightly that the shelves themselves threaten to burst. Office supplies take over all other available spaces. Wires go from printer to computer to cable modem to . . . something you can't figure out because it's impossible to trace the route of the wire. Unopened packages take over the corner. Junk mail mixes with tax forms and school field trip permission slips and old programs for plays, until you can no longer tell what's what. The trash can overflows. You get overwhelmed.

Where do you start? With recognition of the fact that some papers are *not* clutter. You need to devise a method to spot essentials amid the flurry of other trivial paper that floods into your house and separate them immediately, removing them to a particular place until you can act on them, and in a timely way. You need a sorting system.

To find the right sorters and bins and other essential office organizers, you could start by taking a walk down the aisles of an office-supply store (or take your walk in cyberspace by browsing through an office-supply catalog on the Internet). You'll find an incredible wealth of anticlutter tools there.

As you look over what's out there, keep in mind that not every office tool will work in your house. Think about each thing before you purchase it. Take, for instance, a laminating machine. You see it, with a price tag of just $59.95, and it's easy to get carried away with the things you could keep and laminate, rather than throw away: wallet photos that might otherwise get crinkled at the corners; insurance cards; kids' drawings that they've asked you to save; notes and instructions that get left in damp places. What a great home organizing tool, you think. But step back a second and consider: Just how often per year will you actually do any laminating? Do you really want to save everything that your kids might want laminated? Isn't it easier to run to the copy shop a couple of times a year and pay a dollar per laminated sheet? Or just buy a packet of stick-on laminating sheets, rather than a desktop machine? And can you really spare the desktop space? If not, where's the machine going to go?

That's the kind of self-interrogation routine to go through with each potential office item you see: "Will this item truly help me reduce clutter, or is it in itself a form of clutter?" Ask tough questions, not just of big items, such as office machinery, but of small items, such as paper clips: "Can I just buy the standard size? Or do I ever use larger sizes? What about butterfly clips? Or alligator clips? About how often would I use them? If I get them in different sizes, where will I store them? Is it worthwhile getting a dispenser? If so, where will I put it?" And so on. You may discover you need to buy fewer supplies than you first thought. Here's something you may not have considered, but that I highly recommend: a magazine rack—the kind you see in doctors' waiting rooms. This type of wall-mounted magazine rack may be the single most valuable piece of office equipment you can purchase. Why? Just take a look at one and you'll instantly know the answer: It's a place where you can pile papers without creating a pile. You can use the rack to temporarily put mail, school notices, kids' drawings, schedules, newspaper articles, newsletters—pretty much anything you want. Stack up paper on a flat surface and you create a pile that will never become smaller, and in which you'll never find what you're looking for. But with a vertical rack, all your clutter is instantly available to you. And it's not clutter, either!

Heck, you can even assign everyone in your family his or her own slot for whatever purposes your imagination lends itself to.

Let's take a step back for a moment and talk about something that's even more basic to organizing paper, and that offices employ by the truckload: filing cabinets. Filing cabinets are mundane, unexciting things, but oh-so-essential to dealing with paper. I'm willing to wager that the twenty-first-century home (and the twenty-second-century home, should the publisher decide to keep *Outwitting Clutter* in print that long) can't cope without a filing cabinet. If you don't have a filing cabinet in your house, then you probably are already swamped with papers—but it's not too late. Run right out to the office furniture store and bring back a filing cabinet today, or better yet, two.

There are several varieties of filing cabinets to choose from, and what kind you buy probably has more to do with your personal preferences than your level of clutter. If you plan to keep

Wall-mounted rack.

your filing cabinet in a public place or look at it often, you'll want an attractive wooden one. If it's going to be kept in the basement or attic, then a cheap black metal model will suffice. Which brings me to the next issue: Should you keep the cabinet in an accessible place like the family room, study, or corner of your bedroom? Or should it be relegated to the basement, attic, or garage? Here's where your self-knowledge should be the determining factor: If you're the kind of person who's just too lazy to put things away in the basement or attic, then the filing cabinet must be more centrally located. If you put the cabinet in a dark corner of your garage, you may never get around to putting your papers in their proper place, and you might as well not have a filing cabinet. On the other hand, if you can tolerate spending a little time in isolation just filing, then it's okay to put the cabinet in the dark reaches of your house.

Speaking for myself, I feel it's worthwhile to own at least two filing cabinets: one for things I access relatively often, and another for records I hope never to have to see again, but am legally required to keep (my old tax files, for example). One small filing cabinet—the more attractive one—goes in my home office; the other—the big, cheap, ugly, black metal one—is down in the basement utility room.

Next issue: vertical or lateral? That may be a more difficult question to answer than the perennial "paper or plastic?" But I can offer a couple of guidelines. If you're cramped for space, a vertical filing cabinet may be your preferred choice. If you need a flat surface to put other things on (like that laminating machine I warned you about), then pick a lateral filing cabinet.

See how much fun it can be to talk about filing!

Another organizing must: Everyone in the family should have his or her own in-box or cubby. You don't have to buy those ugly plastic in-box/out-box stackers to make in-boxes for everyone. It can be more informal than that, just as long as everyone knows where a message or mail meant for someone else is meant to go. Once you've established the physical spot for each person, then it's up to each to be responsible for checking and maintaining the in-box. If you want to encourage your kids to use this system, that's where their allowance can be put. (But let me suggest that you not take this idea to the extreme: The in-box is not the place where the Tooth Fairy should deposit her gift.)

There is one problem with in-boxes, and that is that they tend to become storage spaces; in other words, in-boxes can become magnets for clutter. Watch out for that.

If you find that happening, then buy a shredder. I'm not kidding. You can get a stand-alone model or the kind that fits on top of your garbage can. Tell members of your family that as soon as anyone's in-box is full to overflowing, you will indiscriminately use the shredder on the stuff to take care of the excess. That ought to get them going. (Of course, if you are the chief offender, you might want to come up with a different approach.)

What else should you get? That's really up to you. Browsing office-supply stores and catalogs is often more productive—not to mention entertaining—than trying to figure out in advance what you need. Keep in mind that most office-supply stores will deliver, too (so you won't have to hire those teenagers whom you befriended, as mentioned in chapter 2).

Messages and Reminders

There are so many different systems you can use to take down and store information such as telephone messages, appointments, directions, and reminders. Not every system works for everyone; in fact, usually only *one* system works for most people, and the hard part is figuring out which system is the right one. Finding a workable note-taking system is like finding a mate. You go through a lot of undesirable systems, and sometimes you don't know that something (or somebody) isn't going to work out until you've spent time and money on it. Sometimes the system (or person) you have works well until an unusual or unexpected situation develops: Your note-taking system might be great until you're appointed to be the top of your son's grade's telephone tree, or your partner might be perfect until you discover that she doesn't share your enthusiasm for nude skydiving.

So give some thought to what system will work best for you. Otherwise you'll have all manner of clutter: envelopes, Post-it notes, et cetera. The important thing is to choose a *single* system. For example, you could use a computer program such as MyCorkboard (www.mycorkboard.com), which turns your computer's desktop into an old-fashioned bulletin board. Or you could actually use a real corkboard.

As a message center for the household, a popular choice is the front of the refrigerator. If you're trying to avoid going to the refrigerator too often, then choose a wall near a frequently used telephone and designate it as the spot for Post-it notes.

When you find something that works, stick with it, resisting the entreaties of others to change over to whatever system works for them. What you really want to avoid is having two or more different systems in use in the same household. That's a sure road to disorganization—and worse: dissension in your family. If you usually put telephone messages on the refrigerator, but then decide that putting Post-it notes on the front hall table is a better system, heaven help you if you don't reveal the new system to everyone else who lives in your house. Hell hath no fury like a teenager who doesn't get her telephone messages.

While your home message center should be standardized, your personal reminder system is something else entirely. When it comes to reminders, many people are quite forgetful. And many people, no matter how potent the reminders, still forget. Let me give you an example of what I mean. There's a couple I know, who shall remain anonymous. But let's call them Jim and Vivian. Jim was going to have back surgery to repair a ruptured disc. The surgery is straightforward and requires just an overnight stay in the hospital. But the pain that prompts the surgery is considerable: On a scale of one to ten, for most people it's a ten. So there's strong incentive to get the surgery done.

There were only two things Jim needed to do to prepare for surgery. First, not eat the night before. Second, remember to bring the MRI (a scan of his spine) that was taken a week before. The surgeon told Jim, "No MRI, no surgery." Consequently, Jim and Vivian left half a dozen Post-it notes reminding them to bring the MRI to the hospital. They also left the MRI film on the bench by their front door. (They had discussed putting the MRI film in their car the night before, but the dismissed that idea, just in case the car was stolen.)

You know already know the ending to this story, I'm sure; otherwise I wouldn't be telling it: Jim and Vivian forgot to bring the MRI film to the hospital. Fortunately, Jim was much more devoted to getting places early than he was about remembering what to bring to places. He and Vivian were at the hospital more than an hour ahead of schedule, plenty of time for Vivian to drive back home and get the MRI film, which was just where they'd left it, on the bench by the front door, screaming with Post-it notes written in bright red ink on orange paper that said, BRING!!!!! DON'T FORGET!!!!!

The moral of this story is that any system you think you have that works, may not work in a pinch. A good backup system is never a bad idea.

Remembering stuff goes hand in hand with clutter. Clutter often makes it difficult for us to see what's important, what we want to remember. I think it's just possible that Jim had so many other Post-it notes around the house he was suffering from Post-it note overload, and just saw right past the one on the front door that said, TAKE MRI TO HOSPITAL. What he really needed was not more notes, but some secondary system, such as a text message preprogrammed to ring on his cell phone in the morning, alerting him to the words on the screen: TAKE MRI.

Technology today has given us a wide range of devices and services to use to deliver such reminders. If you own a cellular phone, you'll probably discover that it has its own built-in calendar with audible reminders you can set. These alarm clocks aren't terribly difficult to program—far easier than a VCR, for instance. If you always carry your cell phone, consider making use of its alarm features.

You can also use a free service that sends reminders to your cell phone whenever you want. This service, HZ, at www.hz.com, is designed to be used by cell phones that can send and receive e-mail messages: You send an e-mail to hz.com with information about when you want to get a message back, and your phone rings at the preselected time. (That's what Jim should have done.)

There are numerous free Internet services that can remind you of important events and activities. Some will even give you advance warning once a year that your anniversary is approaching. Others, such as Mr. Wakeup, can be used to remind you not only of meetings but also of when to take your medicines. Mr. Wakeup, www.mrwakeup.com, reminds you with a voice message that contains the specific information you want to be reminded about. Another similar service is Memo to Me, which sends reminders to your e-mail address or text-based cellular telephone. It's at www.memotome.com. There are still other services that let you put your calendar and reminders entirely on the Internet, such as Magical Desk, www.magicaldesk.com. Many Internet portals also have calendars and reminder services, including Yahoo (www.yahoo.com) and MSN (www. msn.com). Yahoo and MSN will let·you upload information from your computer's calendar. Speaking of your computer's calendar—take advantage of any audible and visual alerts that the calendar you use provides.

And yes, it's okay to use Post-it notes, too.

Pay Your Bills Electronically

You may have heard the line: "There's all this talk about the paperless office. But the paperless office is about as likely as the paperless toilet."

While that's true, you can move a tiny bit closer to a paperless world by paying your bills electronically. And with reducing paper comes reducing clutter. What's more, paying your bills electronically helps reduce the sort of clutter that you can't just throw out as soon as you get it. Magazines, catalogs, and junk mail can be tossed whenever you want, but if you start throwing out the electric company's bill as soon as it arrives to help reduce clutter, just make sure you have ample solar cells. Many different creditors let you set up electronic payments. These include credit card companies, utilities, mortgage companies, and cable television companies. In addition, most banks these days offer electronic bill payments to anyone who otherwise would receive a check from you. Most of these electronic bill payment systems can be integrated with your software banking program, so you can track the payments. There are also online companies, such as PayPal (www.paypal.com), that are simply electronic transfer agents (that is, they're neither your creditor nor your banker). You can open an account, designate the source of funds from which you want the payment to be made, and authorize a check to be sent to anyone you designate. If the payee has a PayPal account, too, you simply authorize the electronic transfer of funds from your account to the payee's account and the money goes instantly, avoiding the "hold" period often imposed by banks on out-of-state transactions.

By paying your bills electronically, you're eliminating not only the incoming clutter but the outgoing clutter, as well. You don't have to deal with checks, stamps, envelopes marked POST OFFICE WILL NOT DELIVER MAIL WITHOUT POSTAGE, pens that don't work, and other paraphernalia. Paying bills online is also faster than paying them the traditional way. These programs keep an electronic copy online for you, so there's less to file. As a final plus, you can review and pay your bills from anywhere in the world, so you don't have to worry about those bills that arrive while you're on vacation.

Some electronic payment programs deduct money directly from your account; others require that you positively authorize the payment. Use what you're comfortable with. Some credit card companies notify you by e-mail that your bill is available online for viewing, giving you the opportunity to dispute any charges.

Going digital can make a big dent in your clutter problems. It also eliminates the worry about undelivered mail.

Technology not only reduces clutter but actually frees you from your desk: From any cybercafé in Oslo, Norway, for instance, you can sip an espresso and take care of the mortgage and American Express. For guides to cybercafés, check out:

www.netcafeguide.com/
www.indranet.com/potpourri/links/cybercafe.html
www.cybercafe.com/
www.cyberiacafe.net/cyberia/guide/ccafe.htm

Digital Clutter

7

The Truth about Technology

This chapter is about clutter on your computer.* You may think that this is an office problem and wonder why this subject isn't a subsection of the previous chapter. It could be, but then computers have become such a big part of our world, and pervade so many aspects of life that I thought only a whole chapter would allow me to cover the issues in their full complexity. Computers aren't like other parts of your house or office that accumulate clutter. The clutter they store exists on a plane of reality halfway between the physical world and the imagination. In the physical world, you may have a photo album, a collection of CDs, a windowsill full of bonsai plants, and a gallery of velvet paintings. Barring a fire or a velvet painting thief, you are unlikely to lose any of these things or forget where you left them.

On the other hand, store things on your computer (or store digital images of the actual things, as you may do for anything you collect) and you could sit down one day in front of your keyboard and mouse and click a few times to retrieve the file, only

---

*Alas, I must admit that some of the information in this chapter is specific to PCs. Mac users, as we all know, live a clutter-free life.

to discover, to your shock and horror . . . it's gone. Vanished. Possibly wiped out forever in a silent but massive computer crash. Or maybe just mysteriously transported from a readable section of your hard drive to some hidden, unreachable, unreadable part of the machine.

It's not a far-fetched scenario. In fact, it's happened to the best of us. Even to a computer maven like me. I present my own missing file case as a cautionary tale. In 1992 I wrote a book called *Baby-English: A Dictionary for Interpreting the Secret Language of Infants*. I make it a habit to keep file copies of all my manuscripts, just in case I need to revise the book or it goes out of print and I want to have the book republished. That's exactly what happened to *Baby-English*.

But when I went to retrieve the file of the manuscript, now very ancient by today's computer standards, it was nowhere on my home computer. It wasn't on my wife's computer, either. Same thing for my office machine: Possibly some enterprising part-time assistant had decided to save space by deleting that file, or perhaps the file containing the manuscript hadn't survived the transition from computer to computer. After all, I wrote *Baby-English* four computers ago.

I wasn't exactly in a panic, but I wasn't relishing having to re-type eighty-six pages of baby talk with numbered definitions in multiple fonts, with frequent use of boldface and italics.

I searched through my entire collection of floppy discs. I searched my Zip discs, even though Zip discs didn't exist when I wrote *Baby-English*. I searched my Jaz drive (a high-capacity removable disc). I looked everywhere, but the original manuscript was nowhere in digital form. Finally—thanks partly to inspiration and partly to desperation—I looked in my daughter's computer. There it was, intact and preserved. You see, we pass down computers in our house, and the kids get the slightly older machines. I have to say that it wasn't easy finding the file, because it was originally saved in a Windows 3.1 format—which, you may recall, doesn't allow file names to be more than eight letters. The file was called babyengl.doc.

Then there was another problem. I had encrypted the file to keep prying eyes from . . . oh, who knows what. It was probably completely unnecessary to encrypt the manuscript, but I did anyway, for some reason that may have seemed important in 1992. Now I had the manuscript, but for the life of me had no idea what my favorite password was back in 1992. I ended up re-typing the entire manuscript. What fun.

The point of this story is that is very, very easy to drop, misplace, and lose track of old computer files. (A few years ago I made hard-drive copies of all my old short stories that were still on five-and-a-quarter-inch floppy discs, while I still owned a computer with a five-and-a-quarter-inch drive.) Unless you (1) organize your computer files and (2) back them up with considerable care and determination, you *will* lose them. That's not Murphy's Law talking; it's just the way technology works.

Backing Up

Let's talk first about backing up your computer files, because that's a simpler question to tackle than how to organize them.

Like houseplants, computer files need regular attention.

More and more of our lives are becoming digitalized. Many people now keep things on computer that were never put in digital form before, including our:

- Photos.
- Movies.
- Address book.

- Calendar.
- Schoolwork.
- Office work.
- Bank book.
- Shopping receipts.
- Music.

In the days before computers it took a significant catastrophe to lose any of these items; now it's possible to lose *all* of these things *at once*, in a fraction of a second, through a computer virus, fire, flood, errant keystroke, cat that decides to take a nap on your keyboard, software bug, faulty installation, hard-disc failure, power surge, theft, or something you never even thought about in the first place. It is absolutely vital to back up your files.

Toward that noble end, I suggest a two-prong approach: Back up locally and off site.

The current technology will dictate which technologies work best, but I have some specific and general suggestions. Among the specific, I happen to like external hard drives. They're fast, reliable, easy to set up, and completely automated. I use a Buslink external USB hard drive that holds sixteen gigabytes of data. (The drive was $250.) The drive came with AutoSave software that automatically copies any file to the external drive as the file is changed or modified. So when I save a word-processing file, for example, a copy of that file is placed on the external drive, too. I like the USB or Firewire external hard drive more than I like backing up on a Zip drive because the USB or Firewire drive holds *everything* I do—there's no swapping discs. It's easier to use than a CD-R (writeable CD disk), because CD-burning software is a little cumbersome. An external hard drive is faster than backing up on tape (which almost nobody does anymore, anyway). And the virtue of the external hard drive is that when—not if, but when—I move into a new computer, I can copy all my files to the new machine with just a few keystrokes.

Another virtue of backing up on a separate hard drive is that the software lets you store multiple versions of your files, so that you can restore not just the version you saved an hour ago, but yesterday's copy. That's a very helpful feature for those occasions when you say to yourself, "I wish I still had that page I wrote yesterday before I deleted it. I really liked that version better."

Whatever system you choose, your backups should be as hassle-free as possible. Backing up data is a little like flossing teeth—nobody really enjoys it, but it is necessary. Don't floss and you could lose your teeth. Don't back up and you could lose your data.

After you start backing up, it's a good idea to make sure you're actually backing up your important files. Often, backup software automatically selects data files, but your software may not select all the files that matter most to you. Many e-mail programs, financial data programs, and personal information managers (the programs we keep our address books and calendars in) use nonstandard file formats. Your software may not back up these files without human intervention. Don't trust your computer.

There's nothing wrong with using a second backup plan, too, such as CD-ROMS, floppy discs, tape drives, Zip discs, or another medium. As I write this book, writeable DVDs are coming. You can never have too many backups.

But keeping your only backups at home is still teasing Murphy's Law. While it's unlikely that you'll lose the data on your hard drive *and* your backup, do you really want to take the chance that your entire life's work could vanish in a millisecond?

Many businesses back up their data to another location. You wouldn't want your bank to keep all its records under one roof, would you? The value of off-site back ups was demonstrated conclusively on September 11, 2001, when the World Trade Center towers came down. Many brokerage firms and other financial organizations lost their main offices—but not their customers' vital records. Those were backed up off site. Nearly all the companies were able to reassure their customers that their money was safe and other branches were able to handle their transactions the very next business day. It's not overstating the case to say that good backup systems are part of what makes us resilient, undefeatable people.

I back up my data to a remote computer in Pennsylvania. Every night, as I sleep, my computer sends copies of all the work I've done for the day to another machine. The files are compressed and encrypted. It's not terribly expensive, either: $160 a year for all I can store. Memory prices are getting lower all the time, too (though computer files are getting larger, as well), so the prices for off-site storage may drop. In addition to the obvious advantage of having a copy of everything in another place should a disaster strike, there's another benefit to off-site storage: You can retrieve your files from anyplace in the world. That helps fulfill your *Mission Impossible* fantasy, in which you have to access your data from a computer in Iraq while enemy agents are closing in on you.

There are numerous free off-site storage services that give you anywhere from ten to one hundred megabytes of space, enough for word-processing, PIM, and financial files, but not enough necessarily for graphics and music files. These include Xdrive (www.xdrive.com), Yahoo (www.yahoo.com), and Driveway (www.driveway.com). There are others, too, and there's no law against using several free off-site backup services. And don't forget the online photo storage and processing companies. Many of these dedicated photography Web sites, such as Photoloft (www.photoloft.com) and Ofoto (www.ofoto.com), will store your pictures for free, in the hope that after you upload your photos to the free Web site, you will order prints from them. These off-site storage services offer password protection, but they do *not* encrypt your data. So your data is subject to a hostile intercept. That only *sounds* cool—if you have your credit card number somewhere in your files, it's definitely a no-no. In other words, use services like Xdrive only for backing up and storing nonsensitive data.

Two commercial off-site storage services you might want to look into are @Backup (www.backup.com) and Connected Backup (www.connected.com.) The advantage of using a commercial off-site storage services, instead of a free one, is that you can store more files on the commercial service. Commercial backup services also use fully automated software, so that your backups involve no work on your part, other than making sure the files you want to back up are included. Off site services are safe for sensitive data. These services encrypt your data before they leave your computer, so not even the company that stores the data can decrypt them.

Pruning and Organizing Your Digital Clutter

Organizing your computer files is a little more difficult than backing them up, but equally important. When your computer gets cluttered with bits and bytes, it's easy for files to get lost, overwritten, and obsolete, which means that while you may still have the file, there's no software around that can read it.

Computer clutter happens all the time, often very rapidly. Friends send you their family snapshots, you bring spreadsheets home from the office, your kids create computer art on your machine, you write a novel, the school e-mails you a class list, or you start converting your CD collection into MP3 files.

Virtually every computer I've ever peered into has a separate folder into which e-mail attachments go, and that folder is a jumble to figure out. Making matters worse, some e-mail programs (I won't name names, but the program maker's initials are MS) have a setting that causes each and every e-mail that's sent to include an electronic Rolodex card. Suffice it to say that the attachments folder is one of the most cluttered folders on everyone's computer.

So start there. Go through your e-mail attachments folder and delete everything that looks worthless, which will be 90 percent of what's there. Not sure if you want the file? Double-click on it (your antivirus software is up to date, right?) to see if the file is something you'd like to keep. If nothing happens when you double-click on that file, that means you probably don't have and never will have the right software to read that file— and it's mostly likely something you can delete.

After looking through the files in your attachments folder for a few minutes, you'll probably discover which kind of files you definitely don't want. Just delete them. For example, files with the extension VFC are those pesky Rolodex cards. While deleting files from your e-mail attachments folder doesn't create the same cathartic feeling as cleaning out your garage, it is nonetheless a very worthwhile thing to do. Hard discs are becoming larger and larger, but the more files you have on your computer, the slower it will run. In addition, more files—just like a big stack of papers on your desk—makes it harder to find the file you really want. If you have a hundred files in your e-mail attachments folder and you're looking for a specific one, you may have a lot of hunting ahead.

Outwitting digital clutter is a two-step process: First get rid of files you don't need (see above); second, organize the files you keep. A good place to start at that task is in a software store (it could be an online store). As is often the case, the software that came with your computer or operating system isn't necessarily the best. Windows Explorer, in my opinion, isn't up to the task of file management, given the fact that a typical computer now has more than ten thousand files on it. Treat yourself to some *good* file management software. I use something called Powerdesk, which you can get at http://www.ontrack.com/software/. Once you have the right software, you're on your way to decluttering your computer.

The principle of good organization of files (not just digital ones, either) is this: Every file should be in its most logical place. Don't just dump everything into a single folder, such as "My Documents," "My Music," or "My Pictures." That's what happens if you let Microsoft Windows pick your file storage place for you. Do you really want Bill Gates telling you how to run your life?

Take it from me, you're much better off creating specific folders and subfolders for particular kinds of projects (see the sidebar for examples). You can use the "My Documents" folder as the master filing cabinet to contain all the specific folders and subfolders you create, if that's the system you're used to. The more specific the folders you have, the easier it will be to find exactly what you're looking for later.

Findable Folders

My Documents
    House Files
        Correspondence
        Contractors
        Ideas
    Novels in Progress

Science Fiction
Children's Stories
Office Projects
Due Right Away
Company Policies
Future Projects
Travel
U.S.
International
My Pictures
Travel & Vacations
School
Business & Insurance Photos
Miscellaneous

Keep an Archive

There's one other "master" folder that I find extremely helpful in reducing digital clutter: "Archives." This is the place to put all the files that you're no longer working on, but may be useful down the road. Unlike physical clutter, which takes up space you need for other purposes, digital clutter isn't all that bad—as long as you control it by keeping it labeled and stored properly. If it's kept in a way that interferes with finding files in current use, then it's a problem, but if it's kept clearly marked as "Archives" then you can hang on to it without much to worry about. You'll even be able to consult files in it, as the occasion warrants. (You might be called upon to settle a bet with something kept in your archives, or perhaps dig out the manuscript of an old, out-of-print book like *Baby-English* that a publisher is offering to bring back into circulation.)

Under your "Archives" folder, you could have subfolders like this:

Archives
   Old Financial Materials (Pre-2000)
   Correspondence 1998–2000
   Old E-mail 1997–2001
   Old Quicken Files 1998–2001

The "Archives" folder is especially helpful when it comes to reducing digital clutter. Definitely create as many subfolders as you think will be helpful in identifying what you've archived. Give these subfolders descriptive names, with dates if that's relevant. It's much easier to figure out what's what when your folder is called "Old Correspondence 1999" than if it's named "Old-Cor9." Typing a bit more doesn't cost you anything, so don't skimp on letters.

There's another benefit to having just a few master folders with many subfolders under them, as opposed to a dozen or more different folders: Backing up files and moving everything into a new computer is much, much easier if all you have to do is move a single folder or just a few. It's less problematic to back up everything in your "My Documents" folder than it is to back up and move the fifteen documents folders you have in different places on your computer. Think of these master folders as moving boxes: Without boxes, moving would be a whole lot more difficult.

Once you have your folders organized, it's also a relatively painless process to move things from an active folder to your "Archives" folder. The "Archives" folder is in my view the key to outwitting digital clutter. After all, nobody needs to have all the computer files, dating back to the beginning of time, or at least the beginning of Windows Me, first edition, in one place. By periodically moving your older files to "Archives," you'll also be more aware of legacy files—those created with obsolete programs that may no longer be readable. By moving files to your "Archives" folder you'll be able to keep them from becoming unreadable and forever lost.

A couple of words of warning are worth repeating when it comes to organizing your digital archives. Digital data have a way of becoming lost—or worse, unreadable—over the eons. What happens if you forget to copy your "Archives" folder to your new computer in two years? Or to your new, new computer in five years? Then your valuable archives are gone.

What if your archived data are no longer readable in ten or twenty years? Photos stored in an old shoe box may become faded, but at least you don't need any special equipment to view them. But your AVI (digital video), DOC (word-processing), or JPG (graphics) files may—and probably will—one day become archaic. If you are preserving files for posterity, for your children, their children, and their children's children, digital may not be the way to go. While my guess is that all these currently popular digital formats will be convertible to whatever format comes into play in the next decade or so, there's no guarantee. So while you are decluttering your life, keep in mind that technology is not always your friend.

Even the much-vaunted compact disc, currently the darling of storage technologies, is on its way to being replaced by DVDs. After DVDs? Who knows.

(If you shrug and think, "There will always be a way to read these old discs and files," here's a dare: Find somebody who can read a Wordstar file on a five-and-a-quarter-inch floppy disc.)

It might be a worthwhile idea to mention your archives in your will. If you are keeping digital information only for your own convenience, then it doesn't matter what happens to your bits and bytes. But if you want your descendants to have what you've so painstakingly collected, make it easy for them.

Five-Minute Exercises in Digital Decluttering

To keep free of digital clutter, spend five minutes a day doing at least one of the exercises below. Since there are five, you could do one for each day of the workweek. There's also useful information on dealing with digital clutter and preventing computer disasters at http://www.adlerbooks.com/prevent.html.

1. **Setups.** Check the setup of your file folders to make sure the folders and subfolders are flexible and fully used. If there are any subfolders that have little in them, integrate them into a larger folder and delete the subfolder. Rename any folders that don't instantly suggest their contents as named now.

2. **Moving around.** Are there any files that aren't where they should be? Browse through your folders in five-minute increments and move any that are misfiled. Be sure not to mess around with any system or program files; just move your data.

3. **Check your backup system.** Even if you use an off-site backup system—and you should—make sure that you're backing up the files you want to back up. Some backup software thinks it knows which files to back up, but trust me, the software isn't all that smart.

4. **Deletion time.** Pick a five-minute period each week (probably at the end of the week) to go through your main file folders and delete what you no longer need. You can do this manually or you can use automated software, such as Norton's Cleansweep.

5. **Clean up the real-world accessories around your virtual reality.** Your computer is your portal into cyberspace but it is also a big, heavy box with a lot of parts. Those parts attract clutter: CD-ROMS, printer switches, external drives, and no end of wires and cables. You do need these things, so you can't simply get rid of them; you just need to keep them in their place. At least once a week make sure all the peripherals that go with your computer are dust-free, tightly connected, and in good working order. Disconnect and take away any accessories that you haven't used within the last month and have no plans to use within the next six months.

Preventing Digital Clutter

There are two steps I recommend to anyone interested in keeping digital clutter at bay. Pruning your e-mail attachment folder, which I described earlier, is one of those. The other is not to use the default folder suggested by the program. Sidekick, a popular personal information manager, puts all its data files in this folder: "\Program Files\Starfish\Sidekick99\Userdata." Eudora, a popular e-mail program, puts its data files (mailboxes) in this folder: "\Program Files\Qualcomm\Eudora Mail\Eudora." What's wrong with that? Well, when a program buries its data several layers down in an obscure folder, it's very hard to back up those files. It's a safe bet that most Sidekick users don't instruct their backup software to back up the files "\Program Files\Starfish\Sidekick99\Userdata*.skcard," which are the address book files. Then when it comes time to move into a new computer, how to do you easily find the files you want to move? The answer is, you don't.

Programmers, aka software engineers, do not know the best way to organize *your* hard drive. Just think for a moment about how they name their folders: "\Program Files\Qualcomm\Eudora Mail\Eudora." Why do they need an extra folder called "Eudora Mail"? And why do many software companies insist on adding a folder for their company's name? It's certainly not to make things easier for you.

But you can make your life easier by specifying a different directory into which to put the program. So instead of "\Program Files\Starfish\Sidekick99\Userdata," my PIM (personal information management) data are in "\Sidekick\Userdata." Makes much more sense, doesn't it?

Many programs let you specify a separate location for their data. No matter where you install the program itself, the data can go into a completely different place.

You might want to create a folder called "Program Data." In this folder should go all the data files for your various programs: e-mail, databases, financial information, PIMs, e-mail mailboxes, and so on. When you back up your data, or just want to find it, you'll know where everything is.

Now and then it's a good idea to walk though your computer's hard drive, folder by folder. Take a look at the folder names. If a folder's name sounds antique or irrelevant, consider deleting it. To reduce the risk of deleting something that you'll actually need, be sure to browse through what's in there to make sure it's no longer useful to you now or in the foreseeable future. (If you suspect it might be, then move it to a more frequently used folder or send it off to your "Archives" folder.)

Sometimes your computer has folders that are mysteries to you. You're not sure what programs they serve or how they got on your hard drive. How do you know if it's safe to delete them? The easiest and fastest way is through the Internet. Post a question about the folder on a few "ask-a-geek" forums and see what answers you get. There are lots of these to choose from; four that I've used with good results are:

Expert's Exchange, www.experts-exchange.com
Help Desk, www.helpdesk.com
PC Service Station, www.pcservicestation.com
Ask-a-Tech, www.ask-a-tech.org

I'm often surprised by the sheer number of junk folders on my computer. Practically anything in your "\Windows\Temp" folder you can get rid of without feeling nervous or guilty. That's where most of your leftover installation files end up. Programs are supposed to clean up after themselves, but then again, so are children. Neither do.

Same thing for files—you need to purge your computer file by file of no-longer-needed matter. (Or is it energy?) My computer has more than eleven thousand files on it, many of which are important, and many of which are about as useful as a broken paper clip. When in doubt about deleting a particular file, it's best to err on the side of *not* (the opposite of the advice, you'll notice, that I generally give when dealing with clutter of the purely physical world).

Besides the "\Windows\Temp" folder, a lot of files wind up in the hard disc's root directory. That's the ":\" folder. Many programs inadvertently save files there—or you do by mistake—and unless you look for them, you'll never know that there are perhaps dozens of files littered around your root folder, taking up megabytes of space. Anyone using a computer with the Windows operating system has files he or she never knew about in the "My Documents," "My Pictures," "My Music," and "My Web Pages" folders. These are folders that Microsoft made the default folders for documents. Look there and see what you find!

There are numerous software packages that help clean up—and declutter—computers. Many of these are "shareware," software you can download for free on a trial basis (typically for thirty days), and can be downloaded from places like Zdnet.com, Cnet.com, and Shareware.com. Others are commercial products such as Norton's Cleansweep, Ontrack's Freespace, and McAfee's disc cleanup utility. All do a reasonably good job; all are safe. And all are important to use if you want to outwit clutter on your computer. Make that *essential*. Having too many files on your computer has the same consequences as having too much junk around the house. You won't be able to find anything you want when you want it—that's the upshot of too much computer clutter. (If you know how to use your computer's file-finding program, computer clutter might not be that much of a problem; still, you don't want to have to waste several minutes doing that every time you're looking for a particular document.)

When you clear out digital clutter, just as with physical clutter, you end up freeing up extra time for yourself to enjoy, as well as making more room for other, more important things.

OUTWITTING CLUTTER TIP

The key to preventing digital clutter is not to let your computer be in charge of how your hard drive is organized.

Friends Don't Let Friends Clutter Their Hard Drives

Somebody knows somebody who has a friend who's added this first somebody to her personal e-mail list. Are you with me so far? In other words, my friend was receiving e-mail from her friend about concerts, lectures, and political musings that my friend's friend thought were important, interesting, or something like that. It wasn't e-mail addressed to my friend; she was getting it as part of a mass e-mailing that went out to dozens and dozens of e-mail addresses. My friend, whose name for the purposes of this book will be "Laura," asked her friend, who shall be called "Beatrice," to take her (Laura) off Beatrice's e-mail list. Makes sense, doesn't it? It's one thing to get e-mail from friends who think you might be interested in stuff that you're not crazy about, but it's another to receive every single e-mail that somebody sends out.

You would think that would be the end of the matter: Somebody asks to be taken off a mailing list and that's that. But in this case, there was a glitch. The glitch was part technological and part personal. Here's the technological part: Beatrice said that it was too difficult for her to organize her e-mail address book to exclude those people who didn't want to receive those mass e-mails. Beatrice told Laura that all Laura had to do was look at the subject line and delete those e-mails Laura didn't want to read.

But Laura didn't want to do that. Laura told Beatrice—no, pleaded with Beatrice—that Laura received so much e-mail that it was really important that she be taken off Beatrice's "friends" mailing list. Beatrice objected again, telling Laura, "You don't understand. It's just too much trouble to selectively remove individuals from my e-mail list. I would have to delete you from my address book entirely."

And then Laura said, "Fine. Delete me from your address book."

Which leads to the personal part. Beatrice had thought that Laura really wanted to get all of Beatrice's e-mails, and was offended that Laura wanted off Beatrice's "exclusive" list. In Beatrice's mind this was like Laura saying "Don't call me; I don't

ever want to hear from you again." Of course it wasn't—it was
more like Laura saying, "Please don't send me your junk mail."
   Why couldn't Beatrice understand why Laura got so ticked
off? Perhaps Laura should have explained it to Beatrice using
real mail as an analogy. Just suppose that every time Beatrice
saw a piece of junk mail or read an article in a magazine that was
of interest to her, she copied it and put it in an envelope and
mailed it off to Laura's house. Sure, Laura could glance at the
return address and see that it was yet another one of Beatrice's
frequent mailings, and toss the envelope out, unread. But Laura
would still have to spend a bit of extra time sorting her mail,
and she'd always wonder, "Maybe this time it's something important." In the real world few people would go to the trouble
of sending their physical clutter to others, but when it comes to
digital clutter, some people think it's okay to clutter up another's computer.
   It may be tough to get yourself taken off somebody's e-mail
list, but that's what you must do. Laura may have been the first
person to tell Beatrice that she would rather be cut out of her
address book than go on receiving digital clutter—but I suspect
she won't be the last.
   If a friend or organization isn't willing or able (actually,
they're always able) to remove you from the e-mail list, you do
have to take matters into your own hands. If you own your own
domain, you should be able to filter all e-mail from a particular
address on your server—that is, the computer that hosts your e-
mail address. Deleting e-mail at the server level is the easiest,
most efficient way to stop e-mail from a particular address from
ever reaching your in-box. If that doesn't work, most e-mail programs give you the ability to filter out e-mail, too. You can create
a filter that deposits e-mail from a particular address right into
your deleted-messages box.

What if the person whose messages you're now deleting wants to send you an important e-mail? Just like most physical clutter you throw out, you can bet that *all* the e-mails that that the Beatrices of the world want to send you are not only less than earth-shatteringly important, but a waste of your time. Will Beatrice be sending you an e-mail that says your kids need to be picked up from school right away? Or that you've been given a promotion at work? Or that there's a hurricane on its way? Nope. Without a doubt, there is absolutely nothing that you need in the way of e-mail from Beatrice. Doubt is often the bedfellow of clutter: Remove the doubt and you have an easier time removing the clutter. If, despite all the pain-in-the-neck e-mails you've received from Beatrice, you still think that she's going to send you something important one day, you'll balk at doing what you must do. So cast aside your doubt and realize that not only can you survive without Beatrice's e-mails, but you'll *thrive* without them.

8

Preventing Clutter

You can't have everything. Where would you put it?
—Ann Landers

Some Good Approaches to Preventing Clutter

Here's the number one way to prevent clutter: Don't have kids.

Oops. Too late.

The second best way to prevent clutter is to keep this thought in mind: It's better to throw something away than to keep it as clutter. "Waste not, want not" is not the ideal philosophy for anyone who's trying to outwit clutter. That old saw is just how it sounds: old. Don't feel that you have to keep something because someone else might say it's wasteful to throw it out. If you don't use it, it's wasteful (of valuable space) to keep it around.

Another good way is to create the space *before* you buy something new. This simple rule can go a long way toward thwarting clutter: If you don't allow yourself the luxury of acquiring a clutter-creating item (and everything creates clutter, right?) until you have a place for it, you stop clutter before it starts.

This is a corollary to the widely observed rule about not buying something unless you have the money at hand. In a way, it's even more important, because when you do make an expensive purchase that's beyond your means, it's often possible to get a loan to pay for the thing. Not so with the space where that purchase will go. A bank or credit union will write you a check, but you can't get a storage company to agree to hang on to your item for free while you work out the space to put it somewhere.

So before you buy, think: "What am I going to do with that new toaster if my old toaster doesn't die as quickly as I'm thinking it might?" If the idea is that you'll just stick it away in a closet somewhere because your kitchen counter already has a bad case of counter-gridlock, and wait until some future time when things somehow "thin out" on their own, you're on the wrong track.

Right track: Donate your old but still functioning toaster to a homeless shelter, or to your neighbor's kid who's going off to college. Or ask yourself, "When was the last time I used that mixed-drink blender to make a banana daiquiri?" and realize that if you gave it away, you'd clear out a nice bit of toaster room right there. Or get rid of that coffee grinder you bought because you thought that fresh-ground coffee would be the perfect way to start the day, only to discover that the coffee grinder's noise makes a leaf blower sound downright enjoyable. Or get rid of that wedding present appliance from your cousin Mel that you never figured out what it was for.

Developing this discipline is not easy, but it is an important part of the ability to outwit clutter. Do things in this order: (1) Clear out the space, and (2) acquire the new object. Succeed, and you'll become a strong anticlutterer. And teach your kids to do this, too.

Expanding on this principle, you should never move a thing from your home to office, office to home, school to home, car to home, or what have you, without a *plan*. Know where you're going to put that thing and you will forever be saved from having framed pictures resting on the floor along your stairwell.

The Barrier Method of Clutter Control

To attack clutter, you often have to deal with the *root* of the problem; you have to stop clutter even before it becomes clutter. You need to pull up weeds to clear out your garden pretty often, but wouldn't you rather just bar the weed seeds from taking hold in the first place? In your garden that means laying down a plastic protective tarp. In your home, what you need is a sort of mental tarp that allows you to bar clutter before it gets through the door.

Let me give you an example of how I do it with CDs. I review new music for an online music service and club called Ecto, which means that periodically I am sent CDs to review. I enjoy reviewing these CDs, but also periodically, I get backed up and I'm not able to review them on schedule. By itself that's not such a clutter calamity, but bear with me for a moment. As I said, one or two CDs resting on top of a stereo doesn't create an undue amount of clutter. Indeed, living in a totally clutter-free world would be boring, so we don't want that either.

So what's the problem? Well, to be perfectly honest, the problem isn't the CDs—it's me. Besides receiving review copies of CDs, I also buy CDs. But I can't shelve the CDs I've purchased until I've finished listening to and writing about the CDs I've volunteered to review. Why? I can't exactly explain why—clutter has both physical and psychological origins, and that's just the way I work. It may have to do with the notion that I can't begin to enjoy my new CDs until I've finished my work. Or with the fact that I feel a need to listen to CDs in the order in which they arrive, so I have to take care of the "review" CDs before the others. The only way I have been able to stop a long train of unshelved CDs from piling up is to bar myself from buying any new CD until I see that my to-review pile has been done. When there's a really great new CD that I'm sure I want in my collection, then I have all the incentive I need to catch up.

Here's a scenario I think many of us have faced: Your good-hearted neighbor with kids a few years older than yours is always dropping off bags of clothing her children have outgrown, assuming that your kids will want them and wear them. But you know full well that about half of what's in the bag will either be rejected by your kids because they don't like the style, or rejected by you because you don't want your kids wearing what clearly look like rags. You're torn between putting up the clutter barrier and refusing to take in the bags and saying, "Thanks, it's very generous of you!" because you don't want to cause a rift between you and the neighbor.*

Well, why not do both? Express your gratitude, by all means, but the instant the neighbor leaves, put the bags of clothing in the trunk of your car. Drive directly to the nearest clothing-for-the-needy drop-off bin. Resist temptation to pick through and remove any clothing that just possibly might be wearable; the minute your neighbor sees your kids wearing her kids' old things, she'll have proof that she's found the right dumping ground for her kids' cast-offs. And absolutely don't let your kids pick and choose from the pile or their closets will *never* be manageable. Get the stuff out before it starts to grow on you, just like some plants in the garden that you're now too tired to weed out.

Same advice for that other neighbor who brings over a thirty-year-old sled, now that her children have long since flown the coop. A sled might be something your kids could use, if it weren't for the fact that (1) your kids already have one, and (2) the one that your children have isn't coated with rust.

In this case, you can't easily get rid of the rusted sled by donating it to charity, because there isn't a charity anywhere that takes horrible, dangerous snow-play vehicles. Yet you still don't want to offend the neighbor by putting the thing out by the

---

*Or else you may find yourself needing *Outwitting Neighbors*, by me.

curb with next week's trash. What do you do? Here's my tactic:
Thank the neighbor profusely for thinking of you even as you
demur, "But my children have far too many things already. I'm
sure there are other kids who really would love and appreciate
this sled more than mine."

Barrier's secure, and you come off as both polite and socially
conscious. More importantly, you have put across the idea that
your neighbor must not think of you or your family as a safe,
easy repository for her clutter.

About Wedding Presents, Birthday Presents, and Other Unsolicited Gifts

Presents, delightful though they may be, are as likely to be clutter as not. Why? Because your friends and relatives seldom know
what you really need. If you're lucky, they can guess what kinds
of things you'd like with about 50 to 60 percent accuracy. But
even things you like can be a form of clutter. You need a strategy
for dealing with the gifts you get, especially if you have a big
event like a wedding or a milestone birthday looming.

It can be hard to readjust our thinking about presents. We're
so conditioned to think of them as wonderful. My reeducation
on the subject began early, when I was in my midtwenties and
had my first book published. That was when I started to get to
know others involved in the book business. When you know
people in the book business, you find yourself frequently receiving copies of their books as gifts. Over the years you can end up
with a *lot* of books this way, books that you would otherwise
never give a second glance in a bookstore, much less buy on
your own.

Let me give you a typical example of this syndrome: I recently
received a book from an author-friend of mine. It was a book on
a subject that I have not a bit of interest in—and will never have

any interest in—but the book was personally inscribed to me. For a few minutes I wandered back and forth between my give-away pile and bookshelf: Where did the book belong? On the one hand, if I kept it, the book would only contribute to my clutter problem. It's not "just another book," but a book that takes the space that might, one day, be occupied by something I really want. On the other hand, what happens if I invite my friend over one afternoon and he happens to mention something in his book (maybe something to do with that personal inscription?) and he asks to see the copy? I may have some fancy explaining to do. Can you guess what I did? (Hint: I did title this book *Outwitting Clutter*, not *Treasuring Sweet Sentiments*.)

A number of years ago my wife (then my bride) and I were faced with a similar, but different, situation. Among the many worthwhile wedding gifts we received was a crystal vase with a trout etched on the side. It really was quite . . . uh, unique. The main problem was that it didn't work particularly well as a vase, which sort of defeated the purpose of owning it. Here's the trouble: A crystal-clear vase looks great until the moment you put flowers in it. Then the water turns murky and mucky, muddy and grubby. What's the point of having flowers if the water they're in looks as though it belongs on the EPA's hit list?

So it was a no-brainer: Get rid of the vase. There was a risk, of course: Our friends might come by some time and expect to see the vase displayed. But that was a risk we were willing to take in the name of outwitting clutter.

So we decided to recycle the vase and give it to another couple as a wedding gift. Shocked? Oh, come on. We wouldn't be the first married couple in the world to recycle a wedding present. Isn't it worse to throw something away?

While we wouldn't be the first people to recycle a wedding present, we might have been caught in the act, which would have been rather embarrassing. The giveaway? The thing was inscribed to us. As I was wrapping the vase, I turned it over for the first time. On the underside of the base, engraved in tiny but quite legible type, were our names and wedding date. The thought of that near faux pas still sends chills down my spine. We would never have been able to face the couple again!

Lesson learned: Giving away to total strangers is a lot less dangerous than giving to good friends.

The point I'm making here is that while it's okay to use, er, creative approaches to giving away presents and other gifts, and even to be aggressive about not letting these gifts clutter up your house, it's important not to really screw things up, as we almost did. So be wary about giving away, exchanging, returning or throwing out a gift if:

1. The person made it.
2. It's inscribed to you. (As you can see, these rules are not written in stone!)
3. It would hurt the giver's feeling forever and ever if he or she found out.
4. There's any likelihood at all that the giver could find out.
5. It could be used as a nice dog toy.
6. You can think of second use for the object, making it very practical. Let me give you an example of what I mean. We received a lacquered music box that plays the much-loved tune "Feelings." (Wo-wo-wo-wo-wo, feee-eelings.) Decorative, but not especially functional, right? Wrong: It turned out that the music box was perfect for revenge against telephone solicitors. When somebody called to sell me something, I would ask them to "hold a minute," then put the phone on the music box and treat them to an endless loop of Wo-wo-wo-wo-wos. That music box was a keeper!

Alternatively, you should keep a database of the gifts you get. Keep them in your address book, or in your computer-based personal information manager. In each giver's entry write down the name of what they gave you, when, and what's unique about it, and the date you mailed them a thank-you note. That way, when your spouse mentions that her rich great-aunt Elmira, whom you haven't seen since your wedding more than a decade earlier, is coming to visit, you can greet her effusively with a line like this one: "Oh, Elmira! We think of you every time we use the fish poacher you gave us. It's the perfect thing for people who love to cook fish." Your relationship with Elmira is now solid enough that you can be sure you'll be remembered in her will, leaving her blissfully unaware of the fact that those "people who love to cook fish" are your new next-door neighbors to whom you gave the fish poacher as a housewarming gift. (And they do indeed invite you over to enjoy fish dinners with them, and you do indeed think of Great-Aunt Elmira with affection every time that happens, and so you've been entirely truthful, to boot!)

There's an advantage to keeping the information in a PIM or some other computer database, as opposed to a handwritten address book: A database instantly lets you find out who gave you what, just by typing "fish poacher" in the "Search" box. A handwritten address book only lets you find presents according to who gave them to you; but sometimes it's useful—or urgent—to find things out the other way around.

Indecision is certainly part of the gift-giving-away process, but you shouldn't let indecision be the cause of your clutter—something that happens all too frequently. Should you return that salad bowl (salad bowl number four)?

You don't have to give away all your less-than-useful presents immediately. Even if you're 99 percent certain that you don't have any need for the fancy porcelain cake display plate, you can keep it for a while—especially if you can store other things inside the cake display plate (that set of hand-tatted lace doilies, for example, that you'll also never use)—until you figure out what to do with it.

Clutter—and especially the clutter of presents given on some big occasion—inexorably encroaches, like zebra mussels or kudzu vines. Clutter will creep into every nook and cranny, unless there's something in its way. Wedding gifts can easily take over your house, weeks before the wedding. Some newlyweds find they don't even have room to move in once the honeymoon is over. If the marriage is to have any kind of future, the couple must first prove they can outwit wedding present clutter together.

Here's the test my new bride and I faced, and passed with flying colors.

We received a set of silver candlesticks as a wedding present. Actually, we got three sets, for a total of six sticks. We exchanged one set at Williams & Sonoma—for a stepladder, as it happens. (I don't know why, but nobody thought to give us a stepladder as a wedding present, even though it's an extremely useful thing, and it folds up very flat, so that it takes up little storage room, thus never contributing to clutter.) We kept the two other sets. One set we keep out on our dining room table and use all the time, because it's very beautiful, and also easy to clean. The other set we keep in our display cabinet in the dining room, because (1) we have room in the display cabinet for it, and (2) there just might come a time when we want to light two different sets of candles. (Can't think when that would be, but the controlling factor here is still "because we have room for it.")

One of these days, many years from now, our two kids will have their own households. And we'll be able to give each of them a set of candlesticks that we can tell them we were given on our wedding day.

OUTWITTING CLUTTER TIP

Elope.

Tell your family and friends, "All we want is your love and your blessing . . . and maybe a nice check."

Buy Things to Store Things

Sound like a contradiction in terms? Actually, it's a pretty sensible move, given that you can't throw everything out or give everything away. And you know when it comes to things like bills, tax documents, medical records, kids' artwork, and many other categories of things, there will always be more coming in. The surest way to prevent these things from becoming clutter is to have a place set aside to put them, the moment they arrive.

But where? You may be able to create the needed set-aside places by clearing away some of the clutter you can do without. If you're like most of us, though, after you clear away clutter, you'll have nice, clean surfaces on your tables, desktops, chairs, and benches, and you'll want to keep them that way. What to do? Acquire some pieces of furniture specifically designed to organize whatever you need organized. You may want to get:

- A mail-sorter hall table (more commonly found in business furniture stores).
- A multicubbyhole desktop hutch to organize home office papers.
- A few different, attractive wooden wall racks (to be used for different purposes in different rooms, such as to organize hats, coats, and scarves in the front hall; spatulas, large spoons and other implements in the kitchen; boots and umbrellas in the mudroom; and car keys by the garage door).

- Media shelves (adjustable for CDs, videos, and DVDs).
- An outdoor bench that doubles as a storage box for outdoor toys.

In addition to furniture, you will also want to look at a variety of products designed specifically as organizers or as storage containers. For these sorts of things you'll want to visit a kitchen-and-closet or bed-and-bath store. Some useful ones are:

- Wrapping paper organizers.
- Holiday trimmings storage bins.
- Stackable toy bins.
- Tool storage boxes.
- Computer supply organizers (including wire-managing tubes).
- Recycling sorters.
- Shoe trees and other types of shoe organizers.
- Hang-from-the-showerhead shampoo racks and suction-cup add-on bath shelves.
- Under-bed rolling storage drawers.
- Spice racks and other pantry organizing systems.
- Shelf doublers (dividing one tall shelf into two shorter ones, or creating a slide-out drawer within a shelf).
- Laundry-sorting hampers.
- Sporting goods racks designed for specific sports equipment.
- Prefab garden sheds designed to store all outdoor supplies.

Hardware stores and general discount stores (like Target or Wal-Mart) also carry a plenitude of organizing products. But if you don't have convenient access to a store with the kind of products you're seeking, then I recommend the Get Organized catalog (800-803-9400, or visit www.shopgetorganized.com).

A Basket Case

Dear Clutter Adviser:

I bought some bottles of wine that came packed in an attractive wicker basket. I finished the wine a long time ago but I don't know what to do with the basket. It's too nice to throw away, but I don't know that I'll ever use it for anything. Maybe it would make a nice picnic basket, but I'm not much of a picnic luncher. Still, I suspect what will happen the minute I get rid of the basket is that I'll be invited on a picnic and will wish I had kept that basket.

Signed,

In Vino Veritas

Dear IVV:

If the basket isn't designed for picnicking—that is, if it's no better than a backpack or a cooler or some other container already on hand that could be used to carry picnic supplies—then get rid of it.

However, I promised at the beginning of this book to come up with new and creative ways to deal with clutter whenever I can, so let me suggest a second solution: Do you have wine paraphernalia, such as extra corkscrews, corks, coasters, metal bottle labels, or any other small odds and ends that you want to keep but seldom use? If you store those items in the basket, then you've turned it into a storage container. Label what's inside it and put it away in a cabinet near your wine rack. So instead of being a piece of surplus acquired because of your wine collection, the basket is now something that helps you organize your hard-to-classify wine accessories.

Yard Sales—The Path to Perdition

Take a walk in the woods. Go cycling. Sew. Rake the leaves. Read a book, or see a movie. Anything but yard sales. Yard sales are addictive to certain personality types. You start out going to one, where you may pick up a bargain or two ("No sweat, I can handle this!"—or so you tell yourself) and then some time later, you go to another, and then a short time after that, another, maybe a bigger one this time—but every time you come away with more and more . . . stuff. At first you're casual about it. You think you're only buying what you can handle. It's just recreational. You can stop anytime. A bit of fun on a Sunday afternoon, that's all it is. Well, maybe on a Saturday, too. But then you realize the best bargains are to be had if you get up early and are the first one to arrive. So you try that. It feels good. Now you're really into it. One day you turn around and realize that you've got closet after closet full of knickknacks and household goods, and things are out of control. That's because yard sales are evil. The devil himself designed them for temptation, knowing we mortals are weak fools.

"Satan, get thee behind me!" was the ancient cry of the exorcist. If ever you feel yourself being tempted, repeat this line under your breath three times while keeping your hands clasped tightly over your zipped wallet or purse. Close your eyes (well, keep them open if you're driving) and continue past the YARD SALE TODAY sign, and you will be saved from Clutter Hell.

The Guest Room Problem (and How to Handle It)

The fortunate among us have a guest room. That's a room that's not inhabited by a permanent member of your household. When my wife and I were married, we had a guest room. We lived in a rented house and didn't have kids (yet). When wedding presents began arriving on our doorstep in large numbers, we didn't know where to put them all, and so for lack of imagination about alternatives, we turned our guest room into a "present room," a place to keep boxes of things we had no idea what to do with (or hadn't gotten around to exchanging for things we really needed).

That was absolutely the wrong thing to do as far as clutter is concerned. A guest room is a highly desirable thing to have, and we squandered that by converting our guest room into Clutter Central.

If you're lucky enough to have a spare room, because you don't have children, your kids have gone to college, or your children have run away with the circus, you need to resist temptation and keep that room available as a guest room or simply an empty space for Zen meditation. It's okay to give a room a particular function, such as an exercise room, study, guest room, kids' playroom, or family room, but it's a big no-no to clutter up a room with, well, with clutter. You can take advantage of the space and put some bookshelves in your exercise room; a stationary bicycle in your family room (maybe even directly in front of the television); a CD storage system in your guest room. In other words, you can piggyback onto a room's function, but whatever you do you should not—wait, make that *must not!*—turn a room, including a basement, into a junk room and nothing more than a junk room. Take it from us: It took more than a year to turn the present room back into usable space.

Now That You've Outwitted Clutter, What Next?

I'm not talking about your next equally ambitious project, such as climbing Mount Everest or taking up hang gliding. Equally difficult might be *keeping* the clutter at bay. When you first moved into your home, it was clutter-free—not unlike what you've accomplished by your own hand—but your house quickly became cluttered. Unless you work hard to hold clutter back, in no time things are going to fall apart.

The most important thing to do is to stop the smallest amount of clutter from being born. I'm not suggesting that you develop an anal-retentive personality, only that you recognize the truth: If you permit any kind of clutter anywhere once you've removed the clutter, you're opening the door to a vicious cycle of more and more clutter. Let's say you've cleaned up your front hall closet and no longer use it for storing cleaning supplies. Then one day you leave a big jug of liquid soap dispenser refiller in that closet, because there's no more room in the cabinet under the sink. What the heck—if there's a bottle of soap, then maybe it's okay to leave a sponge nearby because the soap and the sponge go together and you'll be moving them as one to the cabinet under the sink as soon as some space down there frees up. Soon, there's also a roll of paper towels. And a broom. Without any thought or action on your part, you've got clutter again.

Snowflakes form around a tiny, invisible grain of dust. No dust, no snow. The same principle applies to keeping clutter away after you've outwitted it once. Don't let that initial seed appear. *At all costs* block that first small bit of clutter before it has a chance to grow into a mountain.

Optical Excess

Dear Clutter Adviser:

I'm nearsighted. (I'm also a little overweight, but I guess that's a problem for somebody else.) Here's my problem: Every few years my eyeglass prescription changes. I usually take that opportunity to purchase new frames, to be a little more stylish. But that leaves me with eyeglasses that I can't use because the prescription is out of date. I'm loath to throw those glasses away because the frames were so expensive. But I never wear the old glasses. What should I do?

Sincerely,

Four Eyes

Dear Four Eyes,

The first thing you should do is stop using the word *loath*.

Second, keep a spare pair in your car. If your glasses break and you need them to drive, you'll be very happy that you have an extra pair on hand.

Third, donate the rest. Unlike books, glasses are light and inexpensive to send through the mail. There are several charities that take people's old glasses—with the lenses—and match them to people who need the same prescription. By donating your glasses, you're giving a gift that will truly change somebody's life while decluttering your own. Some eyeglass stores accept donations: You can bring your old glasses into any LensCrafters store, for example. You can find out more about where to donate glasses at The Gift of Sight, http://www.peneyecare.com/donateglasses.htm, or Laser Surgery for Eyes, http://www.lasersurgeryforeyes.com/donateyourglasses.html. Many Lions Clubs also accept donations of eyeglasses.

The Voices of Clutter: 9
Interviews with Real-World Experts, Victims, and Former Clutterholics

Joanne Helperin

Joanne Helperin's desk was hidden underneath piles of paper. Since she converted her living room into a home office, she had watched her desk disappear to the point where she could no longer see the wood. Poor organization and clutter led to misplaced items and a generally inefficient system. She also needed a little help with other trouble spots, such as the kitchen and pantry. Another problem area in the Helperin household was the garage. Helperin thought she was a pack rat until she met her husband, who has about fifteen boxes of memorabilia packed into their garage. Something had to change. Helperin, of Los Angeles, started her search on the Web. She stumbled upon the Clutter Buster Web site and was impressed with the information it had to offer. Once she spoke to the owner, Bob Farkas, she was hooked.

"I didn't know quite what to expect. He's the kind of guy who will go through every piece of paper with you. He will push you to get everything done at that moment. He doesn't believe in 'in the meantime,'" Helperin says.

Helperin believes that hiring a professional organizer was the best thing she could have done. While I personally am a big booster of self-help, I listened respectfully to Helperin explain how her hired expert was able to come up with ideas that would never have crossed her mind. Helperin found that she was more motivated to actually do the work because she was paying for the appointment and he would be coming to see her progress.

Organizing the desk alone took a few days, about three hours of work each day. Farkas questioned her about how often she used some of the items to get a better idea of what she did or didn't need. For example, she had a large amount of paperwork concerning her frequent flier miles. Farkas wrote down all of her frequent flier numbers for all of the airlines and then got rid of all of the other paper. The next step is up to Helperin—she has to enter the information she wishes to save in a file on her computer.

When she finally finished organizing her desk, Helperin felt liberated. "At the end of a session you feel like a weight is lifted off your shoulders. Clutter is an emotional weight," she says.

Among the first lessons she learned through working with Clutter Buster is to keep everything contained by grouping items in buckets, boxes, or other types of containers. She also learned the importance of labeling items in order to avoid digging through containers and making an even larger mess.

Although Helperin has created a sound organizational system, she still has small lapses. She just doesn't let it get to the point where she can't see her desk. When this happens, she calls Farkas for an "emergency trip" and the problem is nipped in the bud.

Here are some useful tips that Joanne Helperin picked up from Clutter Buster:

- If you haven't used it in more than a year, throw it out.
  She had been holding on to a pair of skis for eight years.

The skis were taking up too much space and she knew that she would never use them again.

- Remember that you can always replace the small items. A lot of people fear throwing items out because they worry that they might need them at some point in the future. She had a coupon organizer that she never used. Shortly after she threw it out, she realized that she needed one. Since it's relatively inexpensive, she can simply purchase another one.

- Many items can go inside other items. Packing items within other items is a space saver. You can do this with luggage, handbags, and containers, to name a few. When you purchase an item, always think about whether you can nest it inside another object.

- One of Helperin's favorite tips is about storing plastic bags. She puts hers in a cloth bag that has two elasticized openings (these can be purchased at a florist). You put the plastic bags in the top of the cloth bag, and pull them out of the bottom whenever you want one.

- Helperin is not a fan of specific organizers, such as closet organizers that you purchase in a store or through infomercials. She hasn't had much luck with those because they don't necessarily get rid of the clutter, they just put it in different places.

Bob Farkas

Clutter Buster
Los Angeles, California
310-273-9613 or 310-271-4909

If you lack the time, the strength, the know-how, or the will to clean up your own mess (or any combination of these factors), then hire a professional to do it for you. For those of you who have identified and acknowledged the problem, but can't execute the necessary steps to getting rid of the clutter, there's always the option of calling in a full-time declutterer to tackle the problem.

Bob Farkas owns the Los Angeles–based service Clutter Buster, which serves individuals, families, and groups. The business has been around since 1998, and since that date he has helped many clients organize their lives. The most common culprit he finds in his work is too much paper.

"Paper clutter is the most time consuming and overwhelming, whether it is current paperwork or archived papers that are boxed in a garage. Paper takes so much time and effort to sort through, categorize, and organize that I think it is the most overwhelming to tackle for most people," Farkas says.

He urges clutter fighters to keep in mind that there is a point at which the problematic paperwork can be handled somewhat easily, such as the early stages of accumulation. But once it reaches avalanchelike proportions, he suggests enlisting the help of someone who is (1) professionally equipped to deal with clutter, and (2) far removed from the situation, and so able to maintain objectivity.

Farkas stresses the fact that every case and client is different. There are differences in the type of clutter, whether it's paper, clothes, or furniture, as well as differences in the way clients approach dealing with it. Farkas does a "preliminary walkthrough" with clients who contact him to identify the problem and establish a plan of attack.

"Once I understand where the client is coming from, we dive in and attack one thing at a time, making sure the task is not too overwhelming and frustrating. The first thing I do on each job is to motivate the clients to get rid of a lot of their stuff. Once that has been done we can get on with the process of sorting, categorizing, and organizing what is left," Farkas explains. Farkas provides clients with helpful tips and information to help them maintain the clutter-free habitat he has created for them. For those folks who just can't keep the clutter at bay, Farkas provides clutter maintenance on a weekly basis.

Janet Kitto

Janet Kitto of Edmonton, Alberta, Canada, has had problems with clutter throughout her entire home, including her home office. Kitto can think of only one person who can rival her when it comes to holding on to possessions that should be thrown out: her seven-year-old daughter. "I have a problem letting go of clothes and paper. You name it, I hold on to it. I am a Master Composter/Recycler and I think this is a contributing factor, as I feel like it is more resourceful to reuse an item than to throw it away. I will also admit that I have a fear of letting go. My clutter is a manifestation of that fear," Kitto says.

The excess baggage keeps her from enjoying her life because she is consumed by trying to control it. Like many people, she feels overwhelmed by clutter and finds it difficult to relax.

Once she'd made up her mind to get a handle on her clutter, the first thing Kitto did was read all that she could about getting organized. The knowledge that she's gained has been invaluable and has contributed to her successes. When it comes to raising a child to be organized, the best thing you can do is set a good example, Kitto believes. "Involve the child in the decision and planning process of organizing a room. When a child can see why things go where, it will be easier for her to keep organized. Also, never make organizing a time-consuming project. If it takes too long, no child will keep interested," advises Kitto.

Kitto is a freelance writer and has written several articles about clutter. You can find some of her writings at www.suite101.com/ welcome.cfm/controlling clutter. I particularly recommend her quiz titled, "Are You a Yo-Yo Clutterer?" (aimed at those among us who fanatically clean up a space and then let it become cluttered again in an endless cycle).

Pat Moore

She's called the Queen of Clutter and she's based in McKenney, Virginia. After years in various management positions, Pat Moore decided it was time for a change. It was 1991 and she decided to "do what I love," which meant starting her own personal errand and organizing services. After a year, she decided to stop offering the errand services because she found the organizing more enjoyable and profitable.

Moore specializes in residential organizing. Her work with a client usually begins with a phone call from a distraught clutter victim, typically with an opening along the following lines: "I'm the most disorganized person in the world. I'm ashamed for you to see the mess. I need to clean up before you get here. You won't believe the stuff my spouse/kids have." Regardless of the potential client's approach, Moore usually begins by asking a series of basic questions to determine which areas are the most disorganized and why those areas are posing such a problem, which in turn helps her to figure out what the person would like to accomplish. She also gathers information about the person's lifestyle, the number of people in the home, the size of the home, and goals.

Based on responses to her questions, especially about goals, Moore has found that her clients can be organized into three categories:

First, there are people who just want to get rid of clutter, period.

Second, there are the people who don't want to dispose of anything, but are more interested in finding places and means to store their things in an organized fashion. Third, there are people who are looking for a combination of the two approaches. They want to get rid of some of the clutter, and organize the rest.

Moore has created strategies to work successfully with all three types. She stresses that there is no *one* way to go about organizing a room. If you took two people and asked them to organize a kitchen, they would most likely use two different methods. But each person's different method would probably best serve that person's particular needs. When Moore starts the hands-on phase of her work, the physical organizing of clutter, that's where the information about lifestyle, personality, and goals comes into play. What works for one client may not work for another; each case needs its own analysis—the phase of work the client usually does not see, but is critical nonetheless.

Not everyone can be helped, however, no matter how imaginative the professional organizer may be. In some cases the problem is far too serious to be fixed by the establishment of a new filing system. Sometimes a different sort of professional may be needed—a psychiatrist. Moore recalls one such case that she says was, unfortunately, all too typical:

"I was called by a senior lady who lived in a nice section of town. Goal: to clean off one table so she could invite her grandson over to dinner. I scheduled an appointment. Instinct warned me to call another organizer to help me. The day we get there, the lady was still in her robe, slippers, and curlers. She cracked open the door for us to get in—it wouldn't open all the way.

"As we stepped in the living room there was a path, exactly of vacuum-cleaner width (she had a maid service come to clean!), through the room. Visualize a garden, but instead of plants there are piles of various heights, sizes, and types.

"Walking to the den, I saw a TV. The repairman was there yesterday to fix the remote control. But it wasn't broken—its electronic eye couldn't see through the stacks of magazines (you could barely see the screen). The couch was covered with stuff, with one small butt-sized space where she sat. You could barely see end tables and other furniture peeking out from under stuff.

"We walked through the dining room and the table was covered. As we walked into the kitchen I stopped dead in my tracks. First, the countertops were covered with piles of stuff, up to and blocking the cabinets. All around the floor, against the base cabinets, were bags of groceries. The table was covered with paper (sympathy cards she received when her husband died, several years before). Then there was the electric stove. On one side, covering two burners, was a two-foot- or so high stack of papers, charred on one side. On the other side the back burner had a pile of pots and pans, and the front burner was empty.

"I immediately said our first priority was clearing off the stove. She argued that she needed a table cleared: the stove was okay. I said it was a fire hazard. She said she'd already had two fires and it was okay.

"I peeked in the bedroom and the bed was covered with clothes, except for one side where she slept. I didn't have enough nerve to look in the other rooms.

"The other organizer and I worked like demons all day, well into the evening. We cleared off the stove, both tables, and most of the living room. It was horrible—Tide coupons dating back ten years. The smell was awful; we would carry bags of trash out to my pickup and gasp for air. It was the saddest thing; she was still mourning her husband, and her out-of-town children refused to visit until she 'cleaned up.'

"We left that evening and vowed to not go back. This was not an organizing job, and we felt that our fee was too high for the work required. Emotionally and physically, we were both drained. I contacted several people hoping they could help her, then tried to forget her. But, every time I think about it, I worry, wondering if she got [professional mental] help."

Suzanne Snyder

A mother of three, Suzanne Snyder of Fruitland, Idaho, finds it difficult to maintain domestic order while "chasing her children around" her home. Like many parents, she is perpetually trying to find a healthy balance that allows her to be an attentive parent and an efficient housekeeper. After learning the hard way that she couldn't manage her children and organize her home at the same time, Snyder finally figured out a schedule that works for her. "I find that it is easier for me if I wait until they are asleep at night, and then clean things around the house. It's much easier than trying to do it while I have kids running around undoing my doings during the day. It's also kinds of calming for me to do it when everything is (finally) quiet and settled."

The key for Snyder was to identify what was standing in the way of organizing her home in order to come up with a solution that would work. She devised a schedule in which her children would get her undivided attention during the day, and the dishes and other dirty thing would be dealt with at night. She calls it "delayed multitasking."

The Top Ten Excuses People Give Not to Declutter

10. I have too much work; I'm too busy making a living to work on clutter.

Americans are the most overworked people in the world. For some reason, many of us spend more time at work dotting i's and crossing t's than we do with our families at home. Saying that you don't have time to clean up clutter because you have too much work to do is the same excuse you use for not having time to read in front of the fireplace with your family or throw a Frisbee outside with your kids.

One day, as you face retirement and look back on your life, you'll ask yourself, "Am I really, really glad I spent all that time at the office?" Do yourself a favor and answer the question now, before it's too late to make some changes. Put the question this way: "Wouldn't I get more out of setting aside some time for myself and my family?" Remember, when you spend time getting rid of clutter, you end up with more good things: more space and more time (because you don't have to waste time looking for things or getting duplicates of things you can't find), and you improve relationships within your family (because you're not so annoyed at family members' clutter, once you've all worked together on a decluttering project).

Aren't these things worth more to you than your hourly wage?

9. Things are such a mess here that I haven't the slightest idea where to start.

It would be easy for me to say, start small. Or start with a five-minute project. But that wouldn't help you because you would probably still say, "How?" So instead, here's a thought: Go into a room with a big garbage bag. Crank up the stereo or television if you want. Your only mission is to throw stuff out. Nothing else. If you start with those obvious things that can be tossed, you will be on your way to dealing with other kinds of clutter.

8. I'm not up to the physical challenge of moving heavy stuff around.

Do you have any strong friends, relatives, or neighbors? Throw a decluttering party and invite every helpful, able-bodied person you know. Tell them if they come and lend a hand, they'll get lots of your giveaways to take home for free or sell for their profit (whatever they wish); you'll also provide the food, drinks, and games to liven up the work. Not sure you know enough people who would respond favorably to an invitation like that? Then hire a couple of teenagers with big muscles—that should do the trick.

7. I might need that stuff one day.

That's what you say. Establish a personal rule: If you haven't touched or used something in a specific period of time—five years is a good starting point—then out it goes. By the time you actually need something you haven't used for the better part of a decade, you'll find it either won't work, won't fit (sigh), is obsolete, or is completely out of fashion. (Can you spell *leisure suit?*)

6. I'm too tired at the end of the day to work on my clutter.

Who says that you have to work on your clutter at the *end* of the day? Work on your clutter when you're more energetic. Save the end of the day for something that requires less energy, such as moving furniture around.

Declutter when you're sufficiently enthusiastic, rather than feeling that you have to work on your clutter at a particular time of the day, especially the end of it.

Much of the time, people don't have enough energy to work on their clutter because they don't get enough exercise—they're too sedentary in general. Think of working on clutter as a form of exercise. Decluttering won't make you trim, but it's a lot better for you than Krispy Kreme doughnuts.

5. I've got one big, tough clutter problem I need to deal with first. All the other stuff can wait until I take care of the big problem—but that one is so challenging, I keep putting it off.

This excuse is like writer's block. The only known cure for it is just to force yourself to get down to business. Forget about tackling the big job first. That's a trap you'll never get around. Do what's easiest first, and then move on. Once you get going, you'll find you're on a roll. Save the worst job for *last,* when you have the most experience and the most motivation to get it done (because once you take care of the last job, that's it, you're done!).

4. I'd like to declutter, but other members of my family won't cooperate.

You know what Ann Landers always advises when one spouse complains that the other doesn't want to work on problems in the marriage—and often refuses to recognize that there is a problem? Just do what you can do on your own. That's better than giving up. Pick a part of the house that's your own personal space and deal with that. Once you've shown how much better you can make things by decluttering, odds are good that other members of your family will be impressed. You'll win them over to your way by the practical value of the work you've done. It could well be they just need your good example to get them moving. And even if they don't join in your efforts, at least you've improved your own space. That's a worthwhile end in itself.

3. Working on clutter just isn't fun.

The same can be said about many of the medical exams that people over forty endure every year, but we do it anyway. At least this particular "have-to" is something that doesn't make you pay a deductible. Outwitting clutter is not only free, it can actually make money for you if you resell your unwanted stuff.

But I agree it's not necessarily that much fun. As something that costs nothing, enhances your life, and even helps build stronger bodies, though, decluttering does have much to recommend it. Besides, you can *make* decluttering fun. Declutter with a friend. Declutter naked . . . Better still, declutter with your friend, naked. Listen to music you really like, but haven't listened to in a long time, while you work on your clutter. Put PBS television on in the background and learn about something new, or remember why you hate the Barney song. Reward yourself with chocolate-covered strawberries when you've finished a room.

Unlike driving down the interstate at sixty-five miles per hour, decluttering does not require your full attention. It's a fairly mindless activity. If you make a mistake while decluttering, the consequences aren't all that bad. On the other hand, if you do a great job, the results are so gratifying, you'll never again grumble about how awful the job of decluttering is.

2. What's the point?—it will be just as cluttered in another month.

Start out with a defeatist attitude like that and you're doomed to live in clutter for the rest of your days. But clean up, and as you're cleaning up and putting away each item of clutter, set up a system to deal that type of clutter next time you see it.

You will be able to maintain your clutter-free lifestyle in perpetuity.

1. *I'll do it tomorrow.*

Yes, Scarlett, tomorrow *is* another day, but every day that you put off doing something about your clutter is another day for more clutter to accumulate, until your house looks as if all sense of order has *Gone with the Wind.* In the time it takes you to read that Civil War epic, you could have decluttered half the house (or maybe your whole house, if it's on the smallish side and not too badly cluttered to begin with). Some books lure you to spend time with them that you could have been putting to better use. If you get nothing else from *this* book, let it be the nudge you need to stop putting things off another minute. Put it down right now and get going on that clutter!

Yes, you! And I do mean *now!*

OUTWITTING CLUTTER TIP

Banish the word "tomorrow."

Acknowledgments

No book is an island. Whoever said it was? Books aren't buildings, cars, trees, or mountains either. But they are the product of more than just the author, and it is in this space that the author traditionally recognizes those who helped shepherd the book along, making it a better product in the process. With that in mind, I want to gratefully acknowledge the help and support of my wife, Peggy Robin, who knows a thing or two about words and how they should be put together, and who proved it during *Outwitting Clutter*'s evolution. In the early part of the process, Peggy aptly pointed out that "a book about clutter has to be at least moderately well organized," and when I failed miserably in that department, she fixed things.

Thanks also to Lilly Golden, Lyons Press editor, for helping to shape this book, and to Tony Lyons for his patience and foresight.

I also want to thank the many people who graciously agreed to be interviewed for this book. I would thank them individually here, but I can't seem to find the little slips of paper on which I wrote down their names.

Index

A

Accomplish something, 9
Address book, 68–69
   PIM, 172–173
Adnet.com, 209
Advertising and selling, 52
Age-appropriate toy, 122–123
Alarm clocks, 189
Almanacs, 36
Andre, Carolyn, 147
Anecdotes, xiv, 14, 15–17, 46,
         89–91, 98–99, 150, 188, 216,
         218–219, 228–237
Anticlutter campaign, 178–179
Anticlutter crusade, xvii
Anticlutter goals, x, xii–xiii
Anticlutter projects
   kids, 131–133
Anticlutter rules, 181
Anticlutter tools, 182
Appliances, 214
   electric, 35–36
Archive, 202–205
   folder, 203
Art, 4–5. *See also* Photos
   supplies, 80
A-to-Z organizer, 105–108
Attic, 9
Audible reminders, 189

AutoSave software, 196

B

Baby bathtub, 118
Baby clutter, 115–118
Baby paraphernalia, 116
Baby toys, 130
Backup
   off-site storage services, 199
Backup system, 195–199, 205
Barrier method
   clutter control, 215–217
Baseball caps, 42–43
   decluttering thematic approach,
      75
Basement, 9
Basket, 224
Basketball, 91. *See also* Sports
   equipment
Bathroom, 84–91
Bathtub
   baby, 118
   toys, 125–127
Batteries
   decluttering by theme, 74–76
Bedroom, 9
Bicycle, 94–95
Bills
   electronically, 190–192

Bins, 182
Birthday presents, 109–114, 217–221
BlackBerry. *See* Personal
    information manager
Blankets, 60
Bookmarks, 45–46, 218
Books, 22
    coffee table picture, 39–40
Bookshelves, 131
Boots
    decluttering thematic approach,
    75
Bottles, 84
Boxes, 23
Broken toy management, 122
Brute force, 39–40
    car clutter, 158
Bulletin board, 68
Business cards, 175–176
Buslink external USB hard drive,
    196
Buy things to store things, 222–223

C
Cabinets
    kitchen, 9, 79–84
    storage containers, 129
Calendar, 177, 189
    PIM, 171
Caps, 42–43
    decluttering thematic approach,
    75
Car
    used parts, 22
Car clutter, 156–159
    brute force, 158
    decluttering, 158
    duplicated things, 158
    organizer-type products, 158
    types, 147
Cardboard box bricks, 120–121
Cassettes, 142–149
Catalogs, xiii, 22, 84, 150–151, 190
CD, 142–149, 215
    cases, 45–46

organize, 148–149
    storage, 142–143, 146–148
Cell phone accessories
    decluttering thematic approach,
    75
Cereal boxes, 49
Change. *See* Coins
Charcoal grill, 91
Charitable giveaways, 51
Charity, 52, 216–217
    pickup, 104
Charts
    chore, 133
    kids chore charts
        websites, 133
Childhood, 109–114
Children. *See also* Teenagers
    employ, 93
    involvement, 233, 234, 237
    kid clutter
        strategies for coping, 119–125
    kids chores, 133
    kids outwitting clutter tasks,
        130–133
    kids storage websites, 130
Choices
    limit, 44
Chore charts, 133
Circulars, 63
Clean up
    software packages, 209
Clips, 22, 177, 182–183
Closet, ix, 9
    picture, 27
Closet system
    CDs, 148
Clothes, 36, 216
Clutter
    characteristics, xvii
    keeping at bay, 227
    negative examples, xiv
    spontaneous generation, 15–16
    type to reduce or eliminate,
        176–178
    voices, 229–237

Clutter Buster
  service, 232
  web site, 224
Cluttered housekeeping
  ten rules, 98–100
Clutter problems, xi
Clutter sayings. *See* Sayings related
  to clutter
Clutter-time dance, 7
Clutter-tolerance level, 1–3
Cnet.com, 209
Coat pocket, 9
Coffee table picture books, 39–40
Coins, 22, 80, 131
Collectibles, 4–5, 140–149, 218
Collect recyclables, 132–133
College students, 54
Comfort, 3
Compact disk. *See* CD
Completion, 2–3
Composter, 233
Computer, 194
  accessories
    decluttering thematic
      approach, 75
  clutter, 193–212
  files organizing, 199–202
Connected Backup
  off-site storage services, 199
Control quality, 121–122
Cookbooks, 80
Craft stuff, 140–149
Creative process
  decluttering, 9–11
Credit cards, 155
Cubby, 185–186
Cybercafe
  websites, 192

D
Damaged underwear, 10
Dangerous clutter, 58
Day Runner. *See* Personal
  information manager
Decluttering

car, 158
creative process, 9–11
  plan, 2
  positive experience, 6
  for profit, 51
  by theme, 73–85
  time, 6–11
Defeat clutter
  at starting point, 45–46
Defrosting
  refrigerator, 82
Delayed multitasking, 237
Deletion time, 205
Denial, 25–28
Desk, 224
  drawer, 9
  multicubbyhole desktop hutch,
    222
  organizing, 230
Detergent, 80
Digital clutter, 193–212
  preventing, 206–209
  pruning and organizing,
    199–202
  two-step process, 200–202
Digital decluttering
  five-minute exercise, 205–206
Digital photography, 141
Directories, 79
Discipline, 214
Do-it-yourself IKEA bookshelves,
  145
Donating to charity, 52, 104,
  216–217
Doors
  backs, 66–67
Drawer, 9
  desk, 9
  by drawer, 70
  storage containers, 129
Driveway
  off-site storage services, 198
Duplication, 42–44
  car clutter, 158
DVDs, 146, 197, 204

E

Easy clutter, 19–27
  list, 19–20
Electrical cords, 61, 176
Electric appliances, 35–36
Electronic bill payments, 190–192
Electronic reminders, 167
Elope, 222
E-mail attachments folder, 200
Emotions, 31
Enlisting
  help, 34–35
Excuses
  not to declutter, 239–243
Exercise equipment. *See* Sports
  equipment
Extension cords, 61, 176
External hard drives, 196

F

Farkas, Bob, 231–233
Fasteners, 22
Fast-food toy clutter, 62, 127–129
Fax
  paper
    to e-mail address, 168
Fear
  of getting rid of something, 30
File cabinet, 9, 183–184
  vertical or lateral, 185
File management software
  Powerdesk, 201
Filofax. *See* Personal information
  manager
Findable folders, 201–202
Fire hazard, 236
Flammable things, 60
Foisting clutter, 50–51
Formulate your plan, 2
Forums
  digital clutter, 206–208
  websites, 208
Four-seasons rule, 93–94
Freezer or fridge, 9. *See also*
  Refrigerator

Friends, 40–42

G

Garage, 9
Garage sale, 52, 53, 225
Gas grill, 91
Get Organized catalog
  website, 223
Get Organized Now!, 105–108
Gifts, 217–221. *See also* Presents
  to be wary of giving away, 219
  database, 220
  giving-away process, 220
Giveaway friends, 54–55
Goals, x, xii–xiii, 3
Good clutter, xii
Gracia, Marcia, 105–108
Graham, Neile, 146
Group yard sale, 53–54
Guest room problem, 225–226

H

Hair stuff, 151–154
Halloween candy, 129
Hampers
  storage containers, 129
Handheld computer. *See* Personal
  information manager
Happy Meal toys, 62, 128
Hard drives
  clutter, 209–212
Hard-to-organize clutter, 137
Health
  anticlutter actions, 6–7
Heater, 60
Help
  enlisting, 34–35
Helperin, Joanne, 224–231
Hobby stuff, 140–149
Home message center, 188
Home office, 180–186
Homework overflow, 134–136
House clutter, 57–108
  room by room, 57–73
Housekeeping

cluttered
ten rules, 98–100
Hudson, Phil, 148
Husband. *See* Spouse
HZ, 189

I
IKEA shelves, 145
Important stuff, 97–98
In-box system, 161–164, 185–186
subdivided, 166
Indisputable clutter, 49–51
Information storage
writeable CD disk, 196
Instruction manuals, 137–139
Internet services, 189
Interviews
on clutter, 229–237
Invisible clutter, 166
Items
for return, 169

J
Jumbo toys, 122
Junk mail, 181
Junk Moehlers, 190
Junkyard-dog-mean clutter, 46

K
Keys, 45, 149–150
decluttering thematic approach,
75
Kid clutter. *See also* Children
strategies for coping, 119–125
Kirslis, Marjorie, 98–100
Kitchen cabinet, 9, 79–84
Kitto, Janet, 233–234
Knives, 61

L
Label spaces, 37
Laundry, 131
soap, 80
Lawn chairs, 91
Laziness, 77–78

Lifestyle
know your's, 117
Light bulbs
decluttering thematic approach,
75
Lines
standing in, 8

M
Magazines, 9, 22, 84, 190
rack, 183
Magical Desk, 190
Mailing supplies, 178
Mail-sorter hall table, 222
Management
time, 7–11
McAfee disc cleanup utility, 209
Media shelves, 223
Memories, 31
Memo to Me, 190
Mental checklist, 28
Mental exercise, 71
Message center, 187
Messages, 186–190, 188
Mindset, 11
Miscellaneous, 137
Mistakes, 30–31
Moderation, 133–134
Moore, Pat, 234–237
Motivation, xiv
Mr. Wakeup, 189
MSN
reminder services, 190
Multicubbyhole desktop hutch,
222
Murphy's Law, 197
Music, 141–145
clutter, 149
MyCorkboard, 187

N
National Geographics, 84
Neighborhood giveaway projects,
103–104
Neighborhood swap meet, 124–125

Net hammocks
   storage containers, 129
Newborn clutter, 115–118
Newly divorced, 54
Newlyweds, 54
Newspapers, ix, xiii, 22, 63
Noah syndrome, 94–95
Norton Cleansweep, 209
Notepads, 177
Notes. *See also* Post it notes
   PIM, 171
Note-taking system, 187
Not-so-easy clutter, 23–25
Novels, x

O
Office clutter, 161–192
   rules changing, 178–179
   type to reduce or eliminate,
      176–178
Office organizers, 182
Off-site back ups, 197–199
Off-site storage services, 198–199
Ofoto
   off-site storage services, 198
One Step Ahead
   websites, 130
Online
   selling, 52–53
Online auction, 52
Ontrack Freespace, 209
Optical excess, 227–228
Organic, 92–93
Organizers
   product list, 223
Organizing, ix
   website, 105
Organizing A to Z, 105–108
Outgrown toys, 123–124
Outwitting clutter
   concept defined, ix
   lose weight, 6–7
   reasons, 1–2
   secondary effects, 5–7

P
Packages, 181
Palm Pilot. *See* Personal
   information manager
Pantry, 9
Paper clips, 22, 177, 182–183
Paper clutter, 232
Paper piles, 168
Paperweights, 178
Parenting
   and clutter, 109–136
Pave it, 92
PayPal, 191
Pennies, 22, 80. *See also* Coins
Pens and pencils, 9, 177
Periodic reevaluation, 10
Personal digital assistant (PDA).
   See Personal information
   manager
Personal information manager
   (PIM), 169–173, 206
Personal space, 47
Phone books, 36, 79
Photography course, 65–66
Photoloft
   off-site storage services, 198
Photos, 4–5, 24–25, 45–46,
      214
   digital photography, 141
Physical side
   anticlutter actions, 6–7
Picking up, 46
Pictures. *See* Photos
Piecemeal
   room decluttering, 69–73
Pillows, 43
Pill privacy, 87–88
Plan, 214
   decluttering, 2
Planning step, 2
Pocket PC. *See* Personal
   information manager
Possessions, 11
Posters, 4–5

Post-it note, 68, 167, 173–175, 187, 188
electronically, 190–192
Post-Traumatic Travel Stress Syndrome, 77–78
Pots and pans, 81
Powerdesk
file management software, 201
Prescription drugs, 84
Presents. *See also* Gifts
birthday, 109–114, 217–221
wedding, 217–221
Preventing clutter, 213–228
approaches, 213–214
Prevention, 121
Professional organizer, 229–237
Progressive clutter removal, 32–34
Purses, 154–156

Q
Quantity, 10
Queen of Clutter, 234
Questioning, 71, 182, 214
clutter perspective, 28

R
Racks
storage containers, 129
Receipts, 45
Recipes, 22
Recyclables, 132–133
Recycle, xiii
toys, 127
wedding present, 218–219
Recycler, 233
Reexamination, 10
Reference books, 178
Refrigerator, 9, 66–67, 81–84, 111
defrosting, 82
Refund tickets, 169
Reminders, 186–190
audible, 189
electronic, 167

services, 189–190
MSN, 190
Yahoo, 190
Remotes, 38–39
Residential organizing, 234
Rex. *See* Personal information manager
Right Start
websites, 130
Room, 9
decluttering
ground rules, 72
strategies, 69–73
Rulers, 177

S
Safe-place concept, 67
Safe-place problem, 67–69
Safety
flammable things, 60
Sayings related to clutter
humorous, 14, 193, 239–243
negative, 7, 9, 109, 133, 173, 187, 213
positive, 9, 16, 17, 20, 30, 31, 119, 121, 157, 164, 165, 193, 213, 222
Scan
paper
to e-mail address, 168
Scissors, 178
Self-interrogation routine, 182
Self-questioning, 71. *See also* Questioning
Selling
online, 52–53
time, 52
Sensational Beginnings
websites, 130
Setups, 205
Shampoo bottle blues, 85–87
Shareware.com, 209
Sharp objects, 61
Shelf by shelf, 70

Shelves
    storage containers, 129
Shoes, 43–44, 46
    bags
        storage containers, 129
    clutter, xii
Shovel, 91
Shredder, 186
Sidekick, 206
Signs
    of clutter, 14
Silver candlesticks, 220
Sleds, 91
Snyder, Suzanne, 237
Socks, 45
Software
    AutoSave, 196
    clean up
        software packages, 209
    file management software
        Powerdesk, 201
Sorters, 182
Space, 213–214
    label, 37
    personal, 47
    storage, 121, 186
    tools, 100–102
Sports equipment
    baseball caps, 42–43, 75
    basketball, 91
    bicycle, 94–95
    decluttering thematic approach,
        75
Spouse
    clutter, 12–14
    creates temporary clutter, 63
    personal space, 47–49
    shampoo, 85–87
    sloppiness, 88–91
        example, 89–91
Stacking cubes
    storage containers, 129
Stairs, 58–61
Standing in lines, 8

Staplers, 177
Start small, 32–34
Steak knives, 36
Storage, ix
    CD storage, 142–143, 146–148
    cubby, 185–186
    information
        writeable CD disk, 196
Storage containers, 129–130
    cabinets, 129
    drawer, 129
    hampers, 129
    net hammocks, 129
    product list, 223
    racks, 129
    shelves, 129
    shoe bags, 129
    stacking cubes, 129
    wall organizers, 129
Storage services
    off-site, 198–199
Storage space, 121, 186
Storage towers
    CDs, 142–143, 146–148
Stroller, 116–117, 118
Suitcase, 77–78
Sweater, 45

T
Tape, 177
Target areas, xi
Teenagers, 40–42, 93. *See also*
    Children
Telemarketers, 8
Telephone messages, 187
Television, 8
Temp file, 208
Temp folder, 208
Temporary clutter, 62–65
    alleviate symptoms, 63
Thematic approach
    possible targets, 75
Thematic decluttering, 100–102
Tickets, 169

Time
  chart, 9
  decluttering, 6–11
  frame, 2–3
  management, 7–11
  in traffic, 8
  wasters, 8
Toaster, 214
Tools, 100–102
Touched-paper rule, 164–167
Tough stuff, 137
Toxic materials, 60
Toys, 109–111, 118, 216–217
  age-appropriate, 122–123
  baby, 130
  broken toy management, 122
  fast-food toy clutter, 62, 127–129
  jumbo, 122
  outgrown, 123–124
  recycle, 127
  tub, 125–127
Training
  children, 110–114
Train tickets, 169
Trash bags, 49–50, 156
Trash can, 167
Triage method, 28–29
Tub toys, 125–127

U
Uncluttered past, 57–58
Uncluttered wisdom
  ten pillars, 55–56
Underwear, 10
Unmatched socks, 45
Unopened packages, 181
Unpacking, 77–78
Used car parts, 22

V
Variable visibility, 15
Vase, 50–51, 111, 218–219

Videotapes, 140
Visible
  clutter, 15
Voices
  clutter, 229–237
Volunteering, 8

W
Walk and carry, 46–47
Wallets, 154–156
Wall organizers
  storage containers, 129
Wall racks, 222
Wedding presents, 217–221
Weed patrol, 132
Whole hog
  room decluttering, 69–73
Wife. *See* Spouse
Wires, 176
Workday
  end of, 180
Worry, 7
Writeable CD disk, 196

X
Xdrive
  off-site storage services, 198

Y
Yahoo
  off-site storage services, 198
  reminder services, 190
Yard clutter, 91–94
  ideas, 96–97
Yard sales, 52, 53, 225
Yo-Yo Clutterer, 234

Z
Zen of uncluttering, 5–7